The
COMPANIONS *in Christ*™
Network

www.companionsinchrist.org

So much more!

Companions in Christ offers *so much more* than printed resources. It offers an ongoing LEADERSHIP NETWORK that provides:

➤ Opportunities to connect with other churches who are also journeying through the *Companions in Christ* series.

➤ Helpful leadership tips and articles as well as updated lists of supplemental resources

➤ Training opportunities that develop and deepen the leadership skills used in formational groups

➤ An online discussion room where you can share or gather information

➤ Insights and testimonies from other *Companions in Christ* leaders

➤ FREE *Companions in Christ* posters to use as you promote the group in your congregation

Just complete this form and drop it in the mail, and you can enjoy the many benefits available through the Companions in Christ NETWORK! Or, enter your contact information at www.companionsinchrist.org/leaders.

☐ Add my name to the *Companions in Christ* NETWORK email list so that I can receive ongoing information about small-group resources and leadership trainings

☐ Please send me FREE *Companions in Christ* posters. Indicate quantity needed: (Also available online.)

Name: _____

Address: _____

City/State/Zip: _____

Church: _____

Email: _____

Phone: _____

D1308813

COMPANIONS *in Christ*

Upper Room Ministries
PO Box 340012
Nashville, TN 37203-9540

The COMPANIONS *in Christ* Series

For Lonnette - a servant of Christ fellankin

The Way of
Transforming
Discipleship

LEADER'S GUIDE

Stephen D. Bryant

UPPER ROOM BOOKS®

NASHVILLE

For more information on *Companions in Christ*
call 1-800-972-0433 or visit www.companionsinchrist.org

Contents

Acknowledgments

The original twenty-eight week *Companions in Christ* resource grew from the seeds of a vision long held by Stephen D. Bryant, editor and publisher of Upper Room Ministries. It was given shape by Marjorie J. Thompson, director of Pathways in Congregational Spirituality with Upper Room Ministries and spiritual director to *Companions in Christ.* The vision, which has now expanded into the *Companions in Christ* series, was realized through the efforts of many people over many years. The original advisers, consultants, authors, editors, and test churches are acknowledged in the foundational twenty-eight week resource. We continue to owe an immense debt of gratitude to each person and congregation named there.

Companions in Christ: The Way of Transforming Discipleship is the sixth title in the *Companions in Christ* series. The original twenty-eight-week resource was intended as a foundation for small groups who want to explore the journey of spiritual formation together. Several resources have been developed for groups who want to continue their communities of spiritual formation and growth. Those resources include *The Way of Forgiveness, The Way of Blessedness*, and *The Way of Grace.* More recently *Exploring the Way* was released as a basic introduction to spiritual formation for groups of all sizes, offering a taste of the *Companions in Christ* series. The resource you hold in your hand, *The Way of Transforming Discipleship*, may be used either as a follow-up for the original twenty-eight-week resource or as an introduction to the series. If this is the first *Companions* resource your small group is using, it may create a hunger for ongoing formational experiences in community that the other books in the series could help facilitate. If so, we highly recommend the twenty-eight-week *Companions in Christ* resource.

The articles in *The Way of Transforming Discipleship* grew out of sermons preached by Trevor Hudson at an Upper Room–sponsored event called SOUL*feast* in the summer of 2004. (See www.upperroom.org/soulfeast for information.) The daily exercises in the Participant's Book and the Deeper Explorations in the Leader's Guide are primarily the work of Stephen D. Bryant in consultation with Trevor Hudson with editorial assistance from Eileen Campbell-Reed, who also created the Closing Pilgrimage and Retreat. The work benefited from input by the *Companions in Christ* staff team, which includes Robin Pippin, Kathleen Stephens, Janice Neely, Lynne Deming, and Marjorie J. Thompson. Special thanks to Zena Smith and Sally Havens, who reviewed the early material and gave valuable input.

Introduction

Welcome to *Companions in Christ: The Way of Transforming Discipleship*, a small-group resource designed to help your small group explore and experience the central elements in the journey of discipleship that follows the way of Jesus Christ. The aspects of discipleship that this resource explores include grounding our identity in our belovedness by God, being mentored by Jesus Christ to befriend all the followers of Jesus, listening to the deep cries of pain and hope in our lives and all of creation, experiencing the healing presence of God, and discovering genuine Christian community.

The concluding element of this resource, a Closing Pilgrimage and Retreat, is designed to offer participants a brief pilgrimage into a place of suffering and pain in their own communities. The firsthand encounter with suffering humanity will bring groups face to face with both inward and outward needs and riches. This concluding weekend will also provide retreat time to reflect on the shared experiences of individual and small-group work from the previous six weeks.

In response to small groups who want to continue their exploration of spiritual practices that began with the original twenty-eight-week *Companions in Christ* resource, the Companions in Christ series continues to expand. *The Way of Transforming Discipleship* is the sixth in the series. Earlier titles in the series are *The Way of Forgiveness*, *The Way of Blessedness*, *The Way of Grace*, and *Exploring the Way*.

Each resource in the Companions series expands on the foundational content of the twenty-eight-week resource and uses the same basic format. The foundational resource, *Companions in Christ*, explores the Christian spiritual life under five headings: Journey, Scripture, Prayer, Call, and Spiritual Guidance. Most supplementary volumes of the *Companions in Christ* series explore in greater depth some aspect of one of these primary categories of spiritual practice.

The Way of Transforming Discipleship falls under the Journey heading, as it is an invitation to embrace the journey and enter into the lifelong practice of Christian discipleship.

As in previous *Companions* resources, the approach to scripture is more formational than informational. While scripture provides the context for each chapter's theme, this is not a Bible study in any traditional sense. We will focus on how these stories touch our hearts, move our wills, and shape our spirits to conform more fully to the life of Christ.

About the Resource and Process

Like all resources in the *Companions in Christ* series, *The Way of Transforming Discipleship* has two primary components: (1) individual reading and daily exercises throughout the week in the Participant's Book and (2) a weekly two-hour meeting based on directions in the Leader's Guide. The Participant's Book has a weekly article that introduces new material and five daily exercises to help participants reflect on their lives in light of the article's content. These exercises help participants move from *information* (knowledge about) to *experience* (knowledge of). An important part of this process involves keeping a personal notebook or journal in which participants record reflections, prayers, and questions for later review and for reference at the weekly group meeting. The daily exercise commitment is about thirty minutes. The weekly meeting includes time for reflecting on the past week's exercises, for moving into deeper experiences of spiritual growth, and for engaging in group experiences of worship.

The material in *Companions in Christ: The Way of Transforming Discipleship* includes a preparatory meeting followed by five weekly sessions and concludes with a Closing Pilgrimage and Retreat, which should take place the weekend following the conclusion of Week 5. Following is a brief overview of the content of the sessions.

1. *Knowing Who We Are:* Our true identity is grounded in our belovedness and the blessing of God.

2. *Changing from the Inside:* Jesus Christ invites us to follow him, make him our mentor, welcome all of his followers, accept ourselves in complete honesty, and develop a heart for people.

3. *Listening to the Groans:* Listening to the groans of humanity, of all creation, and of God's own Spirit reveals both intense suffering and profound hope and is central to authentic Christian spirituality.

4. *Experiencing the God Who Heals:* Into the midst of loss and sorrow God offers a mysterious yet powerful healing presence, and followers of Christ are called to participate in God's healing work.

5. *Discovering Community Together:* Discovering and participating in a genuine community of Christian fellowship counters a modern reality in which rugged individualism is highly valued.

Closing Pilgrimage and Retreat: Daily exercises help prepare the group for a pilgrim visit to a site of human suffering; the retreat time will provide space for reflection about the pilgrimage and the previous weeks of small-group spiritual formation.

The Companions in Christ Network

The *Companions in Christ* Network provides a place for sharing conversation and information. The *Companions* Web site, www.companionsinchrist.org, includes a discussion room where you can offer insights, voice questions, and respond to others in an ongoing process of shared learning. Locations and dates for Leader Orientation training events (basic one-day trainings) and the Leader Training events (advanced three-day trainings) are posted here.

The Role of the Small-Group Leader

Leading a group for spiritual formation differs in many ways from teaching a class. The most obvious difference is in your basic goal as group leader. In a class, you have particular information (facts, theories, ways of doing things) that you want to convey. You can gauge your success at the end of the class by how well participants demonstrate some grasp of the information. In a group for spiritual formation, your goal is to enable spiritual growth in each group member. You work in partnership with the Holy Spirit, who alone can bring about transformation of the human heart. Here gaining wisdom is more important than gaining knowledge, and growing in holiness is more important than gaining either knowledge or wisdom. Success, if that word has any meaning in this context, will be evident over months and even years in the changed lives of group members.

Classes tend to be task-oriented. Groups for spiritual formation tend to be more process-oriented. Even though group members will have done common preparation in reading and daily exercises, group discussions may move in directions you do not expect. You will need to be open to the movement of the Holy Spirit and vigilant in discerning the difference between following the Spirit's lead and going off on a tangent. Such discernment requires careful, prayerful listening—a far more important skill for a group leader than talking.

Finally, classes primarily focus on a set of objective data: a Bible passage, information from a book, or analyses of current events. A group for spiritual formation, however, focuses on the personal faith experience of each group member. Each person seeks to understand and be open to the grace and revelation of God. When group members have read and reflected on a scripture passage, the basis for group discussion is not "What did the author intend to say to readers of that time?" but "How does this passage connect to my life or illuminate my experience?" Discussion centers around a sharing of experience, not a debate over ideas. You will model this type of personal sharing with your group because of your involvement in all parts of the group meeting. The type of leadership needed differs from that of a traditional church school teacher or small-group facilitator. As leader, you will read the material and complete the daily exercises along with other members and bring your responses to share with the group. You will lead by offering your honest reflections and by enabling the group members to listen carefully to one another and to the Spirit in your midst.

Leading a group for spiritual formation requires particular qualities. Foremost among these are patience and trust. You will need patience to allow the sessions to unfold as they will. Spiritual formation is a lifelong process. Identifying visible personal growth in group members over the course of *The Way of Transforming Discipleship* may be difficult. It may take a while for group members to adjust to the purpose and style of a formational group process. As a group leader, resolve to ask questions with no "right" answers in mind and to encourage participants to talk about their own experiences. Setting an example of sharing your experience rather than proclaiming abstract truths or talking about the experiences of other well-known Christians will accelerate this shift from an informational approach to a formational process. Trust that the Holy Spirit will indeed help group members to see or hear what they really need. You may offer what you consider a great insight to which no one responds. If it is what the group needs, the Spirit will bring it around again at a more opportune time. Susan Muto, a modern writer on spiritual formation, often says that we need to "make space for the pace of grace." There are no shortcuts to spiritual growth. Be patient and trust the Spirit.

Listening is another critical quality for a leader of a spiritual formation group. This does not mean simply listening for people to say what you hope they will say so you can reinforce them. Listen for what is actually going on in participants' minds and hearts, which may differ from what you expect after reading the material and doing the weekly exercises yourself. While you listen, jot down brief notes about themes that surface. Does sharing center around a particular type of experience? Is a certain direction or common understanding emerging—a hint of God's will or a shared sense of what group members found helpful? What do you hear again and again? What action might group members take together or individually to respond to an emerging sense of call?

A group leader also needs to be accepting. Accept that group members may have had spiritual experiences quite unlike yours and that people often see common experiences in different ways. Some may be struck by an aspect that did not impress you at all, while others may be left cold by dimensions that really move you. As you model acceptance, you help foster acceptance of differences within the group. Beyond accepting differences, you will need to accept lack of closure. Group meetings rarely tie up all the loose ends in a neat package. Burning questions will be left hanging. You can trust the Spirit to bring resolution in time, if resolution is needed. Also be prepared to accept people's emotions along with their thoughts and experiences. Tears, fears, joy, and anger are legitimate responses along this journey. One important expression of acceptance is permission-giving. Permit group members to grow and share at their own pace. Let them know in your first meeting that while you encourage full participation in every part of the process, they are free to opt out of anything that makes them feel uncomfortable. No one will be forced to share or pray without consent. "Where the Spirit of the Lord is, there is freedom" (2 Cor. 3:17).

It is particularly important to avoid three common tendencies:

1. *Fixing.* When someone presents a specific problem, you may be tempted to find a solution and "fix" the problem. Problem solving generally makes you feel better. Perhaps it makes you feel wise or helps to break the tension, but it will not help the other to grow. Moreover, you might prescribe the wrong fix. If you have faced a similar problem, speak only from your own experience.

2. *Proselytizing.* You know what has brought you closer to God. Naturally you would like everyone to try it. You can offer your own experience to the group, but trying to convince others to follow your path is spiritually dangerous. Here is where your knowledge and wisdom come into play. Teresa of Ávila wrote that if she had to choose between a director who was spiritual and one who was learned, she would pick the learned one. The saint might be able to talk only about his or her own spiritual path. The learned one might at least recognize another person's experience from having read about it.

Clarifying and celebrating someone else's experience is far more useful than urging others to try to follow your way.

3. *Controlling.* Many of us are accustomed to filling in silence with comment. You may be tempted to think you should have an appropriate response to whatever anyone says; that is, you may tend to dominate and control the conversation. Here again, patience and listening are essential. Do not be afraid of silence. Your capacity to be comfortable with silence allows you to be a relaxed presence in the group. If you simply cannot bear a long silence, break it with an invitation for someone (maybe one who has been quiet so far) to share a thought, feeling, or question rather than with a comment of your own.

If this style of leadership seems challenging or unfamiliar to you, consider attending a leader training event for *Companions in Christ.* While leadership training is not required to use this resource, it is recommended and encouraged.

Expectations for the Opening and Sharing Insights Sections of Meetings

This section offers a basic process for the first hour of your group session. The first step in the group session is prayer and a time of quiet centering. Invoking the Holy Spirit's guiding presence is especially important in the Opening portion of the weekly group meeting (see "A General Outline for Group Meetings," pages 14–16).

Most of the Sharing Insights part of the group session will focus on individual members discussing their experiences with the daily exercises. Members should bring their journals to refresh their memories of the week's exercises. As the leader, you will want to begin with your own reflections, which sets the tone for the rest of the group. Speak briefly (two to three minutes) in order to allow ample time for others to share. Above all, specifically relate one of your responses to a daily exercise. If your sharing is general or abstract, other participants will be less likely to share personal experiences. Your initial offering in this part of the group meeting is one of your most important roles as a leader. Consider carefully each week what you would like to say, remaining mindful of the role your words can play in establishing group trust and the serious intent of this part of the meeting.

You may also describe and model for the group an approach sometimes called "sharing to the center." The Christ candle set in the middle of the group affirms that Christ is truly the center of all that the group members do and say in the meeting. The living Christ, through the presence of the Holy Spirit, mediates personal sharing. Therefore, participants can share with one another in God's presence by visually focusing on the candle. This focus lessens the need to keep constant eye contact with other participants, which makes revealing deeply personal responses less difficult. The practice also helps the group to sense that God is truly the one with healing answers and guiding solutions, not us.

During the Sharing Insights time, your main job is to listen. Listen primarily for themes—similar experiences that suggest a general truth about the spiritual life, common responses to the readings that might indicate a word God wants the group to hear, or experiences that might offer practical help to other group members as they try to hear and respond to God's call. Take simple notes so you can lift up these themes as the Sharing Insights time comes to an end. You will also ask other group members to share any themes or patterns they may have identified from the discussion. Listen too for key differences in participants' experiences and affirm the variety of ways God speaks to and guides each one of us. Be alert to participants' temptation to fix problems, control conversation, or proselytize. Gently remind them to share only their own experiences or responses. The same guidance applies if a participant mentions someone else, whether in the group or outside it, as an example. Nothing can destroy group trust more quickly than exposing confidences.

By establishing up front some ground rules for group sharing, you may avoid problems. In the Preparatory Meeting, you will explain the various components of each week's meeting. Discuss the nature of this sharing time and establish some basic ground rules for the group. Here are some suggestions:

- Speak only for yourself about beliefs, feelings, and responses.

- Respect and receive what others offer, even if you disagree.

- Listen more than talk. Avoid "cross talk"—interrupting, speaking for others, or trying to fix another person's problems.

- Honor the different ways God works in individuals.

- Do not be afraid of silence. Use it to listen to the Spirit in your midst.

- Maintain confidentiality. What is shared in the group stays in the group. If spouses or close friends are in the same group, they will want to establish outside of meeting time mutually agreeable boundaries to their personal sharing in the group.

- Recognize that all group members have permission to share only what and when they are ready to share.

- Group members have permission to opt out of a process, but not to denigrate it aloud.

You may want to add to this list before you discuss it with the group.

A few minutes before the scheduled end of the Sharing Insights time, state aloud any themes you have noted during the session: a summary report on what you have heard, not a chance to get in the last word. Make it fairly brief: "I noticed that several of us were drawn to a particular passage. I wonder if God is trying to call our attention to something here." This is a time for summarizing and tying together some themes that have already surfaced.

Finally, you may want to close this part of the session with prayer for the deepening of particular insights, for the ability to follow through on the themes or guidance you have heard, for God's leading on questions that have been left open, or for particular situations that have been mentioned. And you may want to invite all group members who are willing to offer simple sentence prayers of their own.

A General Outline for Group Meetings

The weekly group meetings will typically follow the outline explained below. Within the outline are two overall movements: one emphasizes sharing insights and learnings from the week's reading and daily exercises; the other develops a deeper understanding of spiritual disciplines or practices. The first movement, Sharing Insights, is described in the preceding section. The second part of the meeting, called Deeper Explorations, may expand on ideas contained in the week's reading, offer practice in spiritual exercises related to the week's theme, or give participants time to reflect on the implications of what they have learned for their own journeys and for the church. It may include a brief look forward if special preparation is needed for the coming week.

Both movements are intended as times for formation. The first focuses on the group members' responses to the weekly reading and exercises. The second focuses on expanding and deepening the week's theme experientially. Some participants may respond more readily to one part of the weekly meeting than the other. For example, one person may write pages of journal responses to the daily exercises and be eager for the Sharing Insights time but express reticence in joining a group process for the Deeper Explorations. Another person who has had difficulty reflecting on daily exercises may have little to say during the Sharing Insights time but receive great energy and joy from participating in an experiential learning process later in the meeting. Such variations of response may reflect personality types, while other differences may reflect circumstances or life stages in a person's journey. Be patient, accepting, and encouraging of the fullest level of participation each group member can offer.

Consider carefully the setting for your group meetings. An adaptable space enhances group process. One helpful arrangement is a circle of comfortable chairs or sofas. Or participants might want a surface for writing or drawing. Since the group will sometimes break into pairs or triads, plenty of room to separate is also important. Choose a space for meeting that is relatively quiet and peaceful.

A visual focus for the group is important, especially for opening and closing worship times. Some weeks you are free to create this focus in whatever way you choose, perhaps simply with a candle on a small table in the center of the circle.

OPENING (10–15 MINUTES)

This brief time of worship will give group members a chance to quiet down and prepare for the group session to follow. Each group will eventually discover what works best for its members. This Leader's Guide offers specific suggestions; but if you desire, you can develop your own pattern of prayer and centering. Possibilities for this opening worship include (1) singing a hymn together or listening to a selected song on tape or CD; (2) silence; (3) lighting a candle; (4) scripture or other reading; (5) individual prayer, planned or extemporaneous; or (6) group prayer using a written or memorized prayer.

SHARING INSIGHTS (40–45 MINUTES)

The content for this part of the meeting comes from the weekly reading and from participants' responses to the five daily exercises they have completed since the last meeting. If members fail to read the material or skip the daily exercises, they will be left out. If too many come unprepared, the group process simply will not work. Group discussion generally will follow the model given above under "Expectations for the Opening and Sharing Insights Sections of Meetings." Since the Opening has provided prayer and centering time, this section begins with sharing from you as the group leader, continues with group interaction, and ends with a summary, followed by a brief prayer. You will need to keep an eye on the time in order to bring the sharing to a close and have time for the summary and prayer.

BREAK (10 MINUTES)

Group break time serves important physical, mental, and relational purposes. It also offers a chance for snacking if you choose to do that. If so, arrange for someone to provide food. Do not neglect adequate break time, and be sure to take a break yourself as leader.

DEEPER EXPLORATIONS (45 MINUTES)

This part of the group meeting builds on material in the weekly reading and daily exercises. The content is designed to help group members explore in greater depth the weekly theme, generally through scriptural meditation, prayer, creative process, personal reflection, and sharing. This segment of the meeting resembles the experiential part of a spiritual retreat in miniature and requires thoughtful preparation if you are to guide the process comfortably. Please review the leader material early in the week prior to the meeting so that you have time to think through the process and complete any preparation.

CLOSING (10 MINUTES)

As it began, the group meeting ends with a brief time of worship. First you may need to attend to practical matters of the next session's meeting place or provision of refreshments if these vary from week to week. You may also have the group draw names for prayer partners for the coming week and ask for prayer requests.

This guide includes specific suggestions for the Closing. Designed to follow closely the Deeper Explorations, they may include symbolic acts or rituals of celebration and commitment.

Concluding Matters

Song or hymn selections for the Opening and Closing times need careful consideration. Review the hymnals or songbooks available to you, and look for singable tunes with thematically appropriate words. If your group sings reluctantly, locate several audiocassette tapes or CDs to play and invite sing-alongs or simply enjoy listening.

This Leader's Guide suggests songs for each meeting. A number of these come from a songbook entitled *The Faith We Sing* (TFWS), published by Abingdon Press. This recommended resource is ecumenical in scope. It contains songs that represent several worship styles; it is small, portable, and easy to obtain; most songs in it are simple and singable. Abingdon Press now offers a CD with musical accompaniment to every song in the book.

(See the Annotated Resource List in the Participant's Book.) We encourage your group to consider this music resource, while recognizing that each group will have access to different songbooks and may have its own preference. Some songs are referenced (UMH) for *The United Methodist Hymnal*, though they can be found in many hymnals.

The purpose of the Companions in Christ series is to equip persons of faith with both personal and corporate spiritual life practices that will continue long beyond the time frame of any particular resource. Participants may continue certain disciplines on their own or carry some practices into congregational life. Others may desire to continue meeting as a small group. As you guide your group through this journey, you may discover that certain subjects or practices generate interest and energy for further exploration. Some group members may wish that certain readings or weekly meetings could go into more depth. When the group expresses strong desire to continue with a particular topic or practice, take note of it. A number of possibilities exist for small-group study and practice beyond this resource. Some suggested resources are listed on pages 83–89 of the Participant's Book. The group will need to decide future directions toward the end of this experience.

Our prayer for you as a leader is that the weeks ahead will lead you and your group deeper into the transforming presence of Christ. May your companionship with Christ and with one another be richly blessed!

Weekly Needs at a Glance

R eview this Weekly Needs at a Glance list to familiarize yourself with the items needed for *The Way of Transforming Discipleship* Preparatory Meeting and other weekly meetings. Knowing well in advance the needed items will help you avoid last-minute crises.

Weekly Materials

ALL MEETINGS

- Christ candle (large white pillar candle) or other central candle and cloth for worship table
- Hymnals, songbooks, or other arrangements for music (tapes/CDs and player); several options are suggested each week from which you may choose for Opening and Closing
- Extra Bibles
- Group ground rules developed during your Preparatory Meeting, printed on newsprint and posted in your meeting room
- Candle Prayer, printed on newsprint and posted in your meeting room (if you choose to use this prayer as a group):

Light of Christ,
Shine on our path
Chase away all darkness
and lead us to the heart of God.
Amen.

- Newsprint and markers or chalkboard/whiteboard

PREPARATORY MEETING

- Copy of the Participant's Book for each person
- Copies of the Companions *Journal* for those who may wish to purchase one
- A marker and flipchart (or newsprint) with group ground rules written out in advance;
- Sheets of blank paper
- The card "Prayers for Our Way of Transforming Discipleship Group" (in the back of this Leader's Guide)
- Photocopy of each of the tasks of preparation for the Closing Pilgrimage and Retreat (found on pages 76–79 of this Leader's Guide)
- Hymns or songs for the Opening and Closing

WEEK 1 KNOWING WHO WE ARE

- A bowl of water (or two bowls of water, if you have a group of twelve or more)
- A small hand towel (or two, if you have a group of twelve or more)
- The following words on a board or large piece of newsprint displayed so everyone can see: *Remember, (name), you are a beloved child of God!*
- The following scripture references written on the board or on newsprint: Psalm 139; Isaiah 42:1-4; Isaiah 43:1-7; Matthew 3:13-17; Mark 1:9-11; Luke 15:1-7, 8-10, 11-32; Ephesians 1:3-14
- Copies of "My Beloved Charter" on page 37

WEEK 2 CHANGING FROM THE INSIDE

- Blank paper

WEEK 3 LISTENING TO THE GROANS

- A picture of the painting *The Annunciation* (on back flap of Participant's Book), the focus of the Deeper Explorations
- Copies of the Reflection Sheet (page 54) for each participant

WEEK 4   EXPERIENCING THE GOD WHO HEALS

- A stone (or a container of soil)
- A plant (a potted plant or freshly cut flowers)
- A container of water
- A single candle
- A container of oil in a small bowl
- Copies of "A Celebration of the Healing Powers of God" (pages 64–65) for each participant
- Copies of "Christian Practices of Healing" (page 62) and "Quotations about Christian Healing" (page 63)
- The following words on a board or poster paper: *(Name), I anoint you and pray for healing in the name of Jesus Christ. Let this oil soak into your skin, and remind you of the healing love of God.*

WEEK 5   DISCOVERING COMMUNITY TOGETHER

- Arrangements for access into the various areas of your building for the prayer walk
- A planned path through your church building for the prayer walk
- One small candle (a votive will work nicely) for each group member
- One portable candle or small lamp to take with you on the prayer walk
- Information about the Closing Pilgrimage and Retreat (date, time, location, what to bring)

CLOSING PILGRIMAGE AND RETREAT

- Items needed for the Closing Pilgrimage and Retreat can be found on pages 75–88 of this Guide.

Preparatory Meeting

This Leader's Guide to *Companions in Christ: The Way of Transforming Discipleship* directly addresses you, the leader, as it presents the material for each group meeting. In places the Leader's Guide offers suggested words for you to speak to the group as a way of introducing various sections. These words are printed in a bold typeface (such as under the instruction *Set a context*). These words are only suggestions. Feel free to express the same idea in your own words or to adapt as you deem necessary. Remember to speak at a deliberate pace. Whether giving instructions or offering prayers, speaking slowly communicates a sense of peace and grace.

When instructed to guide a reflection process, you will often see ellipses (…). These marks indicate pauses between your sentences to allow participants to ponder them. You will need to develop your own sense of timing in relation to the overall time frame for the guided meditation. Generally fifteen to thirty seconds are sufficient for each pause. In some cases, the text will recommend specific times for certain pauses.

This guide assumes that groups are new to the *Companions in Christ* resources and provides complete explanation of all aspects of the journey. For example, in this Preparatory Meeting, participants carefully review the daily and weekly rhythm and are introduced to the printed resource. If your entire group has experienced *Companions*, feel free to abbreviate familiar material and focus on the distinctive aspects of this resource and your group's process.

PREPARATION

Prepare yourself spiritually. Review the Introduction to the Participant's Book for *The Way of Transforming Discipleship*, as well as the Introduction in this Leader's Guide. Look over the contents page in the Participant's Book so you can answer basic questions about weekly topics (pages 8–9 of this Leader's Guide offers the summary). Pray for your newly forming group and for each of the participants by name. Ask God's guidance for you as you lead and for each group member as together you embark on this spiritual journey.

Prepare materials and the meeting space.

- Set up chairs in a circle with a small center table and Christ candle. Make your meeting space inviting and visually attractive.

- Have a copy of the Participant's Book for each person.

- You will need a marker and flipchart (or newsprint) with group ground rules written out in advance.

- Provide sheets of blank paper for any who did not bring a journal, and the card "Prayers for Our *Way of Transforming Discipleship* Group" (in the back of this Leader's Guide).

- Photocopy one each of the tasks of preparation for the Closing Pilgrimage and Retreat (found on pages 76–79).

- Choose hymns or songs for the Opening and Closing.

Preparation for the Closing Pilgrimage and Retreat. The concluding pilgrimage and retreat experience will involve the entire group in planning the event. Each week the group should talk about how plans are going. The five weeks after the Preparatory Meeting will go by quickly, so stay on top of plans. To help you keep up with this aspect of the process, reminders and suggestions for progress on planning will be offered in this guide each session. To be ready for the preparatory meeting, read the Purpose and Advance Preparation sections of the retreat instructions (pages 73–79), and be prepared to explain the various tasks as you enlist participants to share the responsibility for planning the closing event.

Review the intent of this meeting: To receive a clear grasp of the purpose and process of *The Way of Transforming Discipleship*, to have an opportunity to ask questions and express hopes for the journey, to begin getting acquainted with the group, and to review and adopt group ground rules.

Opening (10 minutes)

Welcome all participants by name as they enter. Be sure that each participant has a copy of the Participant's Book for *The Way of Transforming Discipleship* and a journal or a notebook.

Set a context.

- This meeting will prepare us for a brief journey together over the next six weeks called *Companions in Christ: The Way of Transforming Discipleship.*

- This small-group experience in spiritual formation invites us to explore in a refreshing way what it means to be a Christ-follower, to live an authentic Christian spirituality, and to share the experience with fellow pilgrims.

- As we make this journey, we cannot guarantee transformation, but we will discover many opportunities to open ourselves to the transforming work of God's Spirit and explore both inward and outward dimensions of the Christian journey. We will open ourselves to the voice of God's love, embrace Christ as our mentor, listen deeply to God in the groans of humanity, experience God's healing presence, and discover authentic Christian community.

Provide a brief overview of the Preparatory Meeting.

— A chance for group members to introduce themselves

— Opening worship similar to what they will experience in the Opening of each weekly meeting

— Discussion of the group process

— Discussion of group members' responsibilities

— An experience of the daily and weekly rhythm of *The Way of Transforming Discipleship*

— Closing worship similar to what they will experience in the Closing of each weekly meeting

Ask participants to introduce themselves.

- Ask participants to introduce themselves by saying their name and a few words about what drew them to this group.

- As leader, model by introducing yourself first. Keep your comments brief and simple to encourage others to do likewise.

Join together in worship.

- Invite the group into a spirit of worship:

  As we begin our journey together we want to join our hearts in worship. And as we prepare to enter *The Way of Transforming Discipleship*, we need both a word of caution and a word of grace. The word *transformation* bears a weighty promise. But transformation is not so much a guarantee as a gift, not so much a certainty as a hope that we share in Christ. We will do the work of reading, praying, journaling, gathering, worshiping, sharing, and opening ourselves to God and to each other in the weeks ahead. But the work of transformation is a gift and grace that only God can give us.

- Light a candle as a symbol of Christ's presence in your midst. Say words like these:

  O Christ, we light this candle in the hope and promise that you will be among us along the way of transforming discipleship. Grant us wisdom and courage to open ourselves to your grace.

- Read Romans 12:1-2.

  Listen to Paul's admonition to the Christians at Rome: "I appeal to you therefore, brothers and sisters, by the mercies of God, to present your bodies as a living sacrifice, holy and acceptable to God, which is your spiritual worship. Do not be conformed to this world, but be transformed by the renewing of your minds, so that you may discern what is the will of God—what is good and acceptable and perfect."

- Ask the group to ponder this question:

  What would it mean for each of us to present ourselves as a living offering to God in the days and weeks ahead? Allow a moment of silent reflection.

- Voice a prayer like this one:

  God, our work and worship is to present our selves, our whole beings, as a gift to you. You alone can transform us and renew our hearts and minds. We are grateful for the testimony of scripture, the history of the church, and the companionship of fellow travelers, who bear witness to the amazing transformations of your love and grace. Help us, O God, to join that company of faithful pilgrims.

- Conclude the time of worship by singing together one of these:

    Traditional: "I Have Decided to Follow Jesus" (TFWS #2129)

    Spiritual: "Lord, I Want to Be a Christian" (UMH #402)

PRESENT THE RESOURCES AND GROUP PROCESS (10 MINUTES)

Go over the Introduction in the Participant's Book with group members so that each person understands the process of reading, daily exercises, and journaling, as well as the outline for each group meeting. Here are some items you will want to mention:

Basic flow of the week. Each participant reads the article for the week on Day 1 (the day after the group meeting) and works through the five daily exercises over Days 2 through 6. The group meets on Day 7. Encourage participants' faithfulness to the process. In preparation for the group meeting, suggest that after Exercise 5 they read over their notebook or journal entries for that week.

Basic flow of a group meeting. Explain the various components: Opening, Sharing Insights, Deeper Explorations, and Closing. Summarize for the group the explanatory material found in "A General Outline for Group Meetings" on pages 14–16 of the Introduction in this Leader's Guide.

Materials for each meeting. Ask the members to bring their Bibles, Participant's Books, and journals to each meeting. Because use of the Bible is part of the daily exercises, encourage participants to use a favorite modern translation.

EXPLAIN PARTICIPANT RESPONSIBILITIES (15 MINUTES)

Emphasize the importance of each member's commitment to the daily exercises and practices in making the group process work. If some members have not experienced this type of daily reflection or group interaction, they may need help in feeling comfortable with them. Remind participants: One of the ways we listen to God is by putting our experiences into words. Throughout the week, we record these experiences in our journal. In the group meeting, we articulate what we have recorded. Both processes offer clarity and new perspective.

Present the process of journaling.

Note that some participants may already be experienced in the practice of journaling. Call the group's attention to pertinent points from the material on page 10 of the Participant's Book about the value of recording reflections in a journal or personal notebook. Assure them that the writing can be as informal and unstructured as they want. Because each person keeps notes that are most helpful for him or her, the journal becomes the personal record of the spiritual growth this resource encourages.

Consider the commitment of listening.

Group members also commit to listen to and value the words of others:

As companions together, we give full attention to what God is doing in the life of the one speaking. We learn to listen with our heart as well as our head and to create an accepting space in which all can freely explore their spiritual journeys.

The group becomes a place for deep listening and trusting in God's guiding presence.

DISCUSS COMMON GROUND RULES (15 MINUTES)

Ground rules are explained fully on pages 13–14 in the Introduction to this Leader's Guide. The rules suggested there should prove helpful, but be prepared to offer other possible rules appropriate to the group. You will also want to allow members to make suggestions. Write the completed list on newsprint for the group to see. Remember that the goal is not a formal agreement or covenant but recognition of the basic rules essential for the group to deepen its faith and to mature as a community.

PRESENT PLANS FOR THE CLOSING PILGRIMAGE AND RETREAT (10 MINUTES)

Explain to participants that a significant part of *The Way of Transforming Discipleship* is the Closing Pilgrimage and Retreat. The group will share in planning the retreat under five main areas of leadership: Site Selection, Transportation, Food, Worship Leadership, and Meeting Facilitation. Ask for volunteers to take responsibility for the various tasks. Give them the appropriate photocopied instructions (pages 76–79). The schedule is in the Participant's Book (page 82).

Describe the purpose of the closing event and the necessary advance planning for it to be most effective (see pages 73–74). Lead a brief discussion about possible dates (the retreat should be scheduled the weekend after the last weekly meeting, if possible) and sites for the pilgrimage. Ask the Site Selection person or group to come prepared with specific suggestions next week for the group's consent.

Complete the Prayer Card (5 minutes)

The Upper Room Living Prayer Center and its network of prayer volunteers will begin to hold your group in prayer. Simply fill in and mail the card titled "Prayers for Our *Way of Transforming Discipleship* Group" that is bound into this Guide. Complete the leader's portion of the card by providing your name and your church's mailing address. Please do not use a post office box number. Ask each member of the group to sign his or her first name as evidence of the group's desire to be connected to the larger network of persons involved in *Companions in Christ.*

Break (10 minutes)

Deeper Explorations (35 minutes)

Set a context for experiencing the weekly rhythm of The Way of Transforming Discipleship.

- **In order to get a better taste of the daily and weekly rhythm of *The Way of Transforming Discipleship*, we are going to experience some of the main elements of the week in an abbreviated fashion. This will also give us an opportunity to get to know one another a little better.**

Read an article and do one daily exercise (10 minutes)

- Say in your own words:

  The first thing we do each week is to read the article, and in the days that follow we complete the daily exercises. We are going to do these things now in a brief way.

  1. Invite participants now to take a few minutes to read the preparatory article entitled "Becoming a Christ-Follower" (pages 15–17 in Participant's Book) and then to complete the exercise for reflection that follows.

  2. Encourage them to underline important thoughts and record their insights in their journals.

  3. Provide blank paper to anyone who does not have a journal today.

4. Offer ten minutes of solitary time for reading and reflecting. Participants may remain in their seats or move to a quiet space within the room if they wish.

Share insights (25 minutes)

• Call the participants back to the group. Remind them that this first half of the meeting each week is a time of sharing insights from the articles and daily exercises and naming ways they experienced God's presence during the week. Also remind them that when each person is sharing, everyone else has the important task of listening carefully.

Invite sharing with these two questions:

1. **Briefly, from the article, what stood out for you in Trevor Hudson's story of his journey to becoming what he calls a Christ-follower?** (sharing)

2. **From the exercise, when you have reflected on your own faith journey, what signposts emerged? Try to identify three such signposts from your life's journey.** (After each participant shares, say, "Thank you for sharing your story.")

• Conclude the sharing time by reflecting together about the common themes you heard in the stories.

Closing (5 minutes)

Invite the group to a time of quiet reflection.

What are your hopes for the time ahead of us as companions in Christ? . . . What are your anxieties about these next weeks together? . . . Commit both your hopes and fears to God now in silent prayer. . . .

Offer a brief word of prayer, asking that all might be able to release their hopes and concerns into God's gracious hands. End with thanksgiving for each person and for God's good purposes in bringing this group together.

Close with song. Choose a favorite hymn.

Remind members of their assignment to read the article for Week 1, "Knowing Who We Are," and complete the daily exercises. Also remind them to begin working on their tasks of preparation for the Closing Pilgrimage and Retreat.

Week 1
Knowing Who We Are

PREPARATION

Prepare yourself spiritually. Pray for your newly forming group and each of the participants by name. Ask God's guidance for you as you lead and for each group member as together you embark on this spiritual journey. Read the article for Week 1 and complete the daily exercises, recording your insights in your journal.

Prepare materials and the meeting space.

- Display the ground rules that the group created last week in a place where they can remain throughout the study.

- If you wish to introduce the Candle Prayer (see page 19) in today's Opening time, write it on newsprint or a poster that you can display in future meetings.

- Choose hymns or songs for opening and closing worship times, arranging for song sheets, hymnals, or instrumental accompaniment if you prefer. If you choose to enlist a group member to lead the singing, be sure to ask in advance, so she or he will have time to prepare.

- Set up the room where you will gather so that participants will be seated in a circle, preferably with a small table at the center. The table will serve as an altar space and should be covered with a simple cloth. For today's session place on the table a Christ candle, a bowl of water, and a small hand towel. If you have a large group (twelve or more), you may need to divide participants into two smaller groups for the baptismal remembrance during the Opening time. If so, you will need two bowls of water and two hand towels.

- Write the following on a board or large piece of newsprint and display so everyone can see: *Remember, (name), you are a beloved child of God!*

- Make sure you have enough Bibles for everyone in your group for the Deeper Explorations.

- Write the following scripture references on the board or on newsprint: Psalm 139; Isaiah 42:1-4; Isaiah 43:1-7; Matthew 3:13-17; Mark 1:9-11; Luke 15:1-7, 8-10, 11-32; Ephesians 1:3-14. These verses will be used in the Deeper Explorations time on Beloved Charters. Review the example of the Beloved Charter on page 38 and make enough copies of it and the handout "My Beloved Charter" (page 37) for each participant.

Review the intent of this meeting: To explore more deeply our identity in Christ as beloved children of God.

OPENING (15 MINUTES)

As members gather, greet them by name and extend a welcome to the circle.

Set a context.

> Today we are going to spend some time working with the theme of the first article—thinking about who we really are in God's eyes and why we are here.

Join together in worship.

- Light the candle and say the Candle Prayer together, or offer a prayer in your own words asking for God's guidance and ever-present love in the moments of shared community.

- Listen to the following reading from Isaiah 43:1-3. As you hear the words, begin to remember your own experience of baptism. If you were baptized as an infant or in a time before you can remember, then recall the time of your confirmation or the stories that you were told about your baptism. In what ways was God forming, calling, and loving you through these times? *(Read slowly.)*

> But now thus says the LORD,
>> he who created you, O Jacob,
>> he who formed you, O Israel:
> Do not fear, for I have redeemed you;
>> I have called you by name, you are mine.

When you pass through the waters, I will be with you;
> and through the rivers, they shall not overwhelm you;
when you walk through fire you shall not be burned,
> and the flame shall not consume you.

For I am the LORD your God,
> the Holy One of Israel, your Savior. (Isaiah 43:1-3)

- Allow a few moments for silent reflection.

- Invite participants to remember their baptisms. Offer the following instructions:

   We are going to pass around this bowl of water as a symbol of baptism. When it comes to you, please share a brief memory from the time of your baptism or confirmation (or a remembrance of it as told to you by a family member). Then, whether you remember it or not, say a word about what your baptism means to you. When you are finished sharing, dip your hand into the water, and the group will say to you what is printed on the poster: "Remember, (<u>name</u>), you are a beloved child of God!"

   Begin this remembrance time by going first. Keep your remembrance brief to model for others how they might also share. Pass the bowl, then the towel, to the next person.

   Note: If you have a large group (twelve or more), you may need to divide participants into two smaller groups for this time of remembrance.

- *Sing together.* After everyone has shared a remembrance of baptism and heard the blessing, sing one of the following together:

   Traditional: "Jesus Loves Me" (UMH #191) or "Love Divine, All Loves Excelling" (UMH #384)

   Contemporary: "I Was There to Hear Your Borning Cry" (TFWS #2051)

SHARING INSIGHTS (40 MINUTES)

Remind participants that during the Sharing Insights portion of the meeting, group members identify and share the ways they have experienced God's presence this week. The focus will be on the insights and experiences they had while reading this week's article and doing the daily exercises. Remind the group again of this week's theme: our identity as beloved children of God is central to our journey as disciples of Christ.

1. Ask participants to review the article and the notes they made in their journals. To stimulate thinking you might ask one or more of the following questions *(5 minutes)*:

    • What in the article this week impressed upon you a new insight about Christian discipleship?

    • As you completed your daily exercises, what captured your imagination or opened up an experience of God's presence?

    • What did you discover about barriers to accepting fully that you are beloved by God? What, if anything, did you discover that helps you to overcome those blocks?

2. Invite group members to share insights. Remind them that the task of those listening is to attend fully to each speaker without judging, fixing, or proselytizing. As the leader, begin the sharing time from your own experiences this week. *(30 minutes)*

3. Conclude the time by asking the group to identify common themes they heard in the sharing time. *(5 minutes)*

BREAK (10 MINUTES)

DEEPER EXPLORATIONS (45 MINUTES)

Introduce the theme. (5 minutes)

The focus of this Deeper Exploration is the spiritual practice of holy remembrance—remembering who we are in God, remembering our belovedness. As Trevor Hudson said, *"When we know that we are God's beloved, we have embarked on the journey towards an authentic Christian spirituality."* (page 26, Participant's Book)

One way of remembering who we are in God is by developing for ourselves what has been called a "Beloved Charter."

– A charter is defined as a document delivered by a monarch granting privileges or recognizing rights.

– A Beloved Charter is a statement expressing our belovedness in God drawn from passages throughout the Bible that attest to the fact of our belovedness.

– An example is found on page 38 of this Guide.

– We began to identify Bible verses that speak to us of who we are and why we are here in Daily Exercise 5 this week. You may choose other verses that have special meaning for you.

Explain the assignment.

You began developing your Beloved Charter in Daily Exercise 5 this week.

– Review the guidelines together. If more description is needed, read parts of the Sample Beloved Charter on page 38 of this Guide.

Solitary time for developing a Beloved Charter. (10 minutes)

• Ask participants to use the "My Beloved Charter" handout (page 37) for this.

Share in groups of three or as a whole. (25 minutes)

• Remind everyone of the mystery of community: God's voice is amplified and sometimes speaks to us in new ways as we listen and share. So listen with expectation.

• Invite each person to read the Beloved Charter he or she has developed thus far.

• Following each person's sharing, pause for a moment. Then invite the group to acknowledge what they heard by simply speaking aloud the word or phrase they heard most clearly.

• Remember that anyone is free to pass.

• Before going to the next person, sing one chorus of "Jesus Loves Me" (UMH #191) or another song that everyone knows.

Regather as a group. (5 minutes)

Invite each triad to say a few words about how they experienced this process. Conclude the group sharing by encouraging everyone to post their Beloved Charter where they will see it often, note its significance daily, and see what happens.

Closing (10 minutes)

Ask the group to pause and reflect back over the meeting. Ask:

Where were you most aware of God's presence among us today? What are you going to remember from this week and this meeting?

Invite a silent time of remembering God and gratefully abiding in the love of Christ.

Call for sentence prayers of praise and thanksgiving.

Sing a benediction from the list below or sing again the song you chose for the Opening worship.

> Traditional: "What Wondrous Love Is This" (UMH #292)
>
> Contemporary: "Oh How He Loves You and Me" (TFWS #2108)
>
> Taizé: "Jesus, Remember Me" (UMH #488)

Check plans for the Closing Pilgrimage and Retreat. After the benediction, check in with members to find out if the locations for the retreat and pilgrimage portions of the closing event have been secured. Make sure the transportation planners have the information they need concerning directions and securing vans if necessary. Also check in with Food and Worship leaders to find out if they have questions or need to make any announcements to the larger group.

Handout

MY BELOVED CHARTER

- Review the Bible verses you identified in Daily Exercise 5 or any additional verses that have meaning for you. Which ones speak to you of who you are in God and about what your purpose is?

- Arrange meaningful verses, words, and phrases into a statement. Write it as though God were addressing you by name. It does not need to be lengthy or finished—five or six sentences are sufficient for this exercise, though you may want to develop it more later.

- When you have created something for yourself, spend moments in silence with it, soaking in the meaning and the love conveyed through sacred words.

SAMPLE BELOVED CHARTER

by Trevor Hudson

Trevor, you are my beloved child in whom I delight. You did not choose me but I chose you. You are my friend. I formed your inward parts and knitted you together in your mother's womb. You are fearfully and wonderfully made, made a little lower than the angels, and crowned with glory and honour. You have been created in Christ Jesus for good works which I have already prepared to be your way of life. When you pass through the waters, I will be with you; and through the rivers, they shall not overwhelm you; when you walk through fire you shall not be burned and the flame shall not consume you. You are precious in my sight, and honoured, and I love you. I know all your longing; your sighing is not hidden from me. Nothing will ever be able to separate you from My love in Christ Jesus, your Lord. Abide in My love.

From Trevor Hudson, *Invitations to Abundant Life* (Cape Town, South Africa: Struik Christian Books, 1998), 28–29.

Week 2

Changing from the Inside

PREPARATION

Prepare yourself spiritually. Pray for openness to changes that God may be prompting in you as you work through the articles and daily exercises for Week 2. Be sure to record your insights, feelings, and images in your journal. Pray for your companions on this journey of renewal and hope. Ask for the mind of Christ as you prepare to lead the weekly meeting.

Prepare materials and the meeting space.

- Set up the room where you will gather with seating in a circle, preferably around a small table at the center covered with a simple cloth that will serve as an altar space.

- For today's session, place on the table a Christ candle.

- If you plan to use the Candle Prayer (see page 19) in today's Opening, display the poster you made last week.

- Choose hymns or songs for Opening and Closing worship, arranging for song sheets or hymnals and instrumental accompaniment if available. If group members are reluctant to sing, you might invite them to sing along with a tape or CD of Christian music.

- Familiarize yourself with the Deeper Explorations, which uses the spiritual practice of sacred reading (*lectio divina*). More about *lectio divina* can be found on page 45.

Review the intent of this meeting: To listen deeply and carefully to what it means to be mentored by Jesus Christ and to look for signs of transformation in our lives, including being changed from the inside out, accepting the friends of Jesus, seeing ourselves in all honesty, and cultivating a heart for people.

OPENING (15 MINUTES)

Greet members by name as they gather.

Set a context.

> This week we are focusing on the change that is fashioned in us by God when we decide to become followers of Christ. That change is an ongoing process in which we are shaped and molded by the teaching, caring, and mentoring offered to us by the living Christ.

Join together in worship.

- Light the candle and say the Candle Prayer together, or offer a prayer like this (in your own words):

> God, open us to ever-new transformations of our hearts, minds, lives, and relationships as we attempt to live honestly as genuine Christ-followers and to befriend others in the name of Christ.

- Listen to the following quote from Agnes Cunningham, and reflect silently on the questions that follow:

> "In the life of a disciple, the discriminating screening and weighing of what might be an obstacle in the way of our conformity to Christ in the Spirit is a never-ending process. The attentive eye, the 'eye of the heart,' must be washed constantly of anything that might diminish its transparency or clutter its emptiness."[1]

> As we consider what it means to be followers of Christ and center ourselves in this time of worship, sharing, and deeper exploration, let us ask ourselves these questions:

> – What obstacles might be blocking my path to following Christ?

> – What needs washing from my heart so that I may respond more readily to God?

> – What clutter distracts me from seeing my purpose more clearly?

- Allow a time of silent reflection; then invite one-word responses to this question:

> **What would you most like to let go of?**

> After participants have had a chance to respond with one word, pray a prayer for letting go:

God, help us to empty ourselves of distractions and clutter. Give us courage to let go of anything blocking our way, and clear our hearts so that we are more responsive to you.

- *Sing together* one of the following hymns or a song of your own choosing.
  Traditional: "Living for Jesus" (TFWS #2149)
  Contemporary: "Spirit of the Living God" (UMH #393)
  Taizé: "Live in Charity" (Ubi Caritas) (TFWS #2179)

SHARING INSIGHTS (40 MINUTES)

In the Sharing Insights portion of the meeting group members identify and share the ways they have experienced God's presence this week. Key to this sharing time are the insights and experiences participants had while reading this week's article and doing the daily exercises. Remind the group again of this week's theme: being changed from the inside out and transformation that includes the mentorship of Christ and companionship with other followers.

1. Ask participants to review the article and the notes they made in their journals. *(5 minutes)*

2. Invite group members to share insights from the reading. Remind participants that our task, whether in sharing or listening, is always to be listening for the prompting of God's Spirit. Begin the sharing time from your own experience this week. *(30 minutes)*

3. Conclude the time by asking the group to identify together what they sensed during the sharing time that seemed to be the prompting of God's Spirit. *(5 minutes)*

BREAK (10 MINUTES)

DEEPER EXPLORATIONS (45 MINUTES)

Introduce the theme. (5 minutes)

In this Deeper Exploration, we explore more deeply what it means to allow Jesus to be our lifelong mentor, especially through the practice of prayerful meditation on scripture. In Trevor Hudson's words, "We are on the way of transforming discipleship when, first, we allow Jesus Christ to be the ultimate point of reference for our lives. Jesus says, 'Follow me.' In other words, he asks us to become his students, his learners, his apprentices. He becomes our mentor" (pages 33–34, Participant's Book).

Set a context for reflection about the mentorship of Jesus. (10 minutes)

Discuss the following ideas, using the follow-up question:

How do we allow Jesus to mentor us?

- The Resurrection stories seek to answer the question for the early church, "How do we continue to follow Jesus when he is no longer with us in the flesh to see and hear?"

- The early disciples learned that although Jesus of Nazareth was crucified on a cross and died, the risen Christ continued to be present to them in a variety of ways, as mentor and guide in the way that leads to life. (See, for example, Matt. 28; Luke 24; Acts 1:1-8.)

- The apostle Paul talked about the continuing presence as "Christ in you," the Risen Lord leading us and forming us from within as individuals and communities of faith. (See, for example, Rom. 6:23; 8:1-2, 10-11.)

- One way that Jesus Christ mentors us—individually and in community—is through regular prayerful meditation on scripture (or what is called *lectio divina*). Through this means of grace, Jesus Christ is no longer limited to teachings and memories from the past; he comes alive for us as a real Presence who guides, encourages, and calls us into the Way here and now.

- Scriptural meditation involves reading the text with our eyes and ears, *reflecting* on what it means for us in our minds, *responding* in our hearts to what we hear Christ personally saying to us, and *resting* our spirits in Christ's hands with resolve to be and do as we are directed.

An Exercise in Scriptural Meditation (lectio divina) on John 21:1-8 (25 minutes)

We will focus on a Resurrection story, which is similar in theme to the calling story in Mark 1 that we worked with over the last few days in the daily exercises.

First reading: Reading (encourage participants to listen with faith and expectation, as though for the first time)

Before you read, say:

> **As you listen, pay attention to one thing that stands out for you—a single word, a phrase, an image, or an action. After I've finished reading, continue to focus on what you heard for a few moments in the silence that follows.**

- Read slowly, pausing between sentences, to allow listeners time to hear and absorb the words.

- Pause for a few moments of silence at the end of the passage.

- Go around the circle and invite persons to respond (or pass) with a single thing they heard—a word, phrase, action, or image.

Second reading: Reflecting (pondering possible meanings, personal connections, or words that touch us)

Before you read, say:

> **As you listen this time, be open to where the story has meaning for you, connects with your life, or touches you in some way.**

- Read slowly, pausing now and then in natural places, to allow listeners to hear each word and phrase.

- Pause for a few moments in silence to allow everyone to dwell further on the reading.

- Go around the circle again, inviting persons to respond (or pass) by naming the connection they are sensing to their own life.

Third reading: Responding (to however we hear Christ addressing us personally—with a question, an insight, a call, or a direction)

Before you read, say:

> **As you prepare to listen this final time, ask yourself, *Where do I sense in my heart Christ's presence in an invitation, a calling, or a challenge?***

- Read slowly as before.

- Pause for a few moments in silence to allow everyone to dwell further on the reading.

- Invite persons to share their responses in groups of three.

- Remind participants to give time for each person to share while others listen.

Group reflection. (5 minutes)

Regather the large group and ask:

> **What gift or challenge have you received through this exercise?**

CLOSING (10 MINUTES)

Say in your own words:

> **One of the gifts of allowing Jesus Christ to be our mentor is the way he feeds us spiritually through stories of his life and conversations with the disciples. Let's hear now the next episode of this resurrection story.**

Read John 21:9-14. Ask the following questions, giving time for reflection:

- **How has this experience fed you?**
- **In what way does it leave you hungry?**

Invite everyone into a time of offering sentence prayers of thanksgiving and supplication.

Sing together as a benediction one of the following, or a song of your own choosing:

Traditional: "Guide Me, O Thou Great Jehovah" (UMH #127)

Spiritual: "Just a Closer Walk with Thee" (TFWS #2158)

Contemporary: "Open Our Eyes" (TFWS #2086)

Check plans for the Closing Pilgrimage and Retreat. After the benediction, touch base with everyone to find out how plans are coming for the Pilgrimage and Retreat. Ask the following questions:

- **Is the site chosen?**
- **Has the contact person agreed to a schedule and plans for a meal?**
- **Are transportation and scheduling issues being adjusted to allow time for each part of the weekend?**
- **What help do planners need?**

Leader's Note

MEDITATION ON SCRIPTURE (*LECTIO DIVINA*)

We start by reading a Bible passage to take in its content and contours, to hear the words clearly, and to observe the characters in action. We go on to reflect on possible meanings and to ponder connections with our lived experience in the world. Then we respond in prayer, sharing our thoughts with God and listening for God to speak to us. Finally, we rest in the word or grace that God gives us, acknowledging what we have received with thanksgiving.

The basic flow can be described in four words:

> *Read*
>
> *Reflect*
>
> *Respond*
>
> *Rest*

The process can and should take many creative forms, depending on the passage and the listener. Yet the basic elements of the process remain fairly constant as trustworthy means of searching beyond the surface of scripture and opening our lives to the searchlight of God's love.

Lectio is a key practice throughout the *Companions in Christ* series. The daily exercises call us to meditate on scripture in relation to daily life and the themes of this course. The weekly meetings continue this dynamic as we share together the "daily bread" God gives us and practice scriptural meditation and listening prayer in company with one another.

Week 3
Listening to the Groans

PREPARATION

Prepare yourself spiritually. Pray for an openness of heart, mind, and hands. As you read articles and complete the daily exercises for Week 3, tune your ears to the deep groans of your own heart as well as the hope and pain of others and the whole of creation. Be sure to record your insights, feelings, and images in your journal. Pray for the participants on this journey of renewal and hope as they sit next to their own "pool of tears" this week. Ask for God's guidance as you prepare to lead this week's group meeting.

Prepare materials and the meeting space.

- Set up the room where you will gather with circular seating around a small table at the center covered with a simple cloth.

- For today's session, place on the table a Christ candle and a picture of the painting *The Annunciation,* which will be the focus of the Deeper Explorations. (Painting is found on inside back flap of Participant's Book.)

- If you plan to use the Candle Prayer (page 19) in today's Opening, display the poster.

- Choose hymns or songs for opening and closing worship, arranging for songbooks, instruments, or recorded music.

- Make copies of the Shoe Prayer Reflection Sheet on page 54 for each participant.

- Lead yourself through the Shoe Prayer exercise on pages 51–52 in advance of the meeting.

Review the intent of this meeting: To listen deeply and prayerfully to the groans of humanity, of ourselves, and of God, and to pray with the Spirit in intercession.

Opening (15 minutes)
Welcome participants by name as they gather.

Set a context.

> This week we have been considering the deep pain, grief, and woundedness of the world, our neighbors, and ourselves. We focus on listening as the key that links the inward and outward dimensions of the spiritual journey. Listening to the groans of humanity, of our lives, and of God calls on all our senses to be alive, awake, and attuned.

Join together in worship.

- Light the candle and say the Candle Prayer together, or offer a prayer like this (in your own words):

  > God, we are gathered today to listen to the deep sighs of human hearts and your Spirit. Sharpen our senses so that we might perceive both the hope and pain of creation, and your deep care and concern as Creator.

- Tell about the following moment of prayer: Kristen Johnson Ingram writes about prayer as sometimes being and sometimes doing, sometimes needing words and sometimes calling for feeling. She describes a time when *seeing* became her prayer. She was photographing a wild calypso orchid when she zoomed in with her camera. She says, "I noticed tiny white flowers on the moss, flowers that were invisible to the naked eye. They were so pearly, so perfect, unseeable except to one another, that I began to weep with awe. The prayer of the eye needs no words because what we see dances straight through our whole brain and nervous system and imprints forever on memory and spiritual life."[1]

- Say in your own words:

  > Today we want to open our senses and our holy imaginations to this kind of careful apprehension of the world in all of its hope and suffering.

- Sing together the hymn "Open My Eyes, That I May See" by Clara H. Scott, or speak the words and give a moment for silent reflection after each verse.

  > Open my eyes, that I may see
  > glimpses of truth thou hast for me;
  > place in my hands the wonderful key
  > that shall unclasp and set me free.

Refrain:
Silently now I wait for thee,
ready, my God, thy will to see.
Open my eyes (ears, mouth), illumine me,
Spirit divine!

Open my ears, that I may hear
voices of truth thou sendest clear;
and while the wavenotes fall on my ear,
everything false will disappear. *(Refrain)*

Open my mouth, and let me bear
gladly the warm truth everywhere;
open my heart and let me prepare
love with thy children thus to share. *(Refrain)*[2]

After a time of silent reflection, invite brief responses to the questions:

  – **In what ways do you need opening?**

  – **What is your greatest challenge to deep listening?**

• Invite participants to offer sentence prayers, asking God's assistance toward openness.

Sing together one of the following hymns or a song of your own choosing.
Traditional: "Open My Eyes, That I May See" (UMH #454)
Spiritual: "Nobody Knows the Trouble I've Seen" (UMH #520)
Taizé: "Kyrie Eleison" (Lord Have Mercy) (UMH #484), or
"Stay with Me" (TFWS #2198)

Sharing Insights (40 minutes)

In this portion of the meeting, group members are invited to share experiences of God's presence this week. Insights and experiences from the article and daily exercises of the week are an important part of the sharing. Remind the group again of this week's theme: Listening to the groans of humanity, creation, and even God's own Spirit reveals both intense suffering and profound hope, and is central to an authentic Christian spirituality.

1. Ask participants to review the article and the notes they made in their journals. *(5 minutes)*

2. Invite group members to share insights from the reading. Ask them to focus on *both* the hope and the suffering they discovered this week. Remind them that everyone sits next to a pool of tears. Our work as listeners is to attend to the deep suffering and hope of one another. Start the sharing time from your experience this week. *(30 minutes)*

3. Conclude the time by asking the group to identify together what they heard during the sharing time that seemed to arise from the Spirit. *(5 minutes)*

BREAK (10 MINUTES)

DEEPER EXPLORATIONS (45 MINUTES)

Introduce the theme. (5 minutes)

The focus of today's Deeper Exploration is listening prayerfully to someone you've encountered this week through an exercise in intercessory prayer.

Reflect on listening. (2 minutes)
First, ask the group to hear these words again from the article:

Listening is that key [to an authentic Christian spirituality] and the basis for all Christian ministry and mission. It's the key to healing, evangelism, pastoral care, community building, and peacemaking. It links the inward and outward journeys. It saves us from a false inwardness. Listening helps us to love God with all our heart, soul, mind, and strength. It helps us to love our neighbors even as we seek to love ourselves. Listening can help us in all these ways. (page 44, Participant's Book)

Ask:

What do you respond to in this statement?

Invite the group to ponder the role and mystery of listening as revealed in the painting *The Annunciation* that depicts Mary as she is impregnated by the Holy Spirit through her ear. Place it where everyone can see it. Ask everyone to turn to the inside back flap of the back cover of the Participant's Book. (10 minutes)

- Present the painting.

- Briefly explain the nature of religious art, using the words of Madeleine L'Engle: "Religious art transcends its culture and reflects the eternal. . . . Sometimes when we [look deeply], we are led into places we do not expect." And, "In art, . . . we are helped to remember some of the glorious things we have forgotten."[3]

- Invite the group to reflect briefly together on what they see and on some of the "glorious things" revealed in the painting that they may have forgotten.

- Ask participants to sit in silence before the painting, looking deeply into the eternal that is reflected there and letting it reflect back on them.

- After three minutes of silence, ask the group to share in response to these questions:
  - **What do you see in the painting?**
  - **What did the painting see in you?**
  - **How have you experienced this mystery: being given new life through your ear, that is, your listening?**

Lead the Shoe Prayer exercise. (10 minutes)

The Shoe Prayer, an experience in listening empathetically to another, leads us into intercessory prayer and compassion.

As we have already seen,

- Listening increases our capacity for compassion.
- Through listening, we can enter with Christ into the world of another.
- We can identify with another, stand in his or her shoes, and be a means of grace to him or her through a genuine ministry of solidarity, prayer, or service.

Directions:

- Invite everyone to think about someone they encountered this week outside the "bubble" of their normal routine, perhaps someone they listened to, feel drawn to, or need to pray for. That person will be the focal point of the exercise. As they consider this person . . .

- Get the group in a circle, preferably unobstructed by a table. Move the table, if it is still there from the Opening worship.

- Guide the group step by step through this exercise. Allow time at each step for the participants to enter into the experience. Watch them for clues as to when they are ready to move on. *Say:*

1. **First, take off your right shoe and put it in the middle of the circle.**
2. **Now take someone else's shoe from the middle and put it on your right foot as best you can. When the time comes, that shoe will represent the world of the**

person you feel drawn to intercede for, not the owner of the shoe but the one you listened to this week or need to pray for—someone in your life God wants you to love. Your left shoe (still on your foot) will represent you and your world.

3. Now we can begin. I invite you to begin by focusing your attention on your own left shoe. Your left shoe represents your world. It's a sign of walking in your own world. Think about what it's like to be you, to stand in your shoes, to experience life through your skin.... What are the groans of hope and pain within you? ... Take a deep breath and give thanks for the gift of your life and who you are in God.

4. Now turn your attention to that person you encountered this week whom you want to listen to, love more deeply, or come closer to. When you feel ready to join the Spirit of Christ in attending to the other person, focus your attention on your right shoe.... Try to enter imaginatively into what that person thinks and feels, what it's like to walk in his or her shoes. Ask God to help you to be open to what his or her life is like from the inside.... Listen to the groans within this person's body and spirit, groans of pain and hope....

5. Now imagine how the Spirit might be praying within that person. Where does he or she need to feel the touch of God's healing hand? The apostle Paul writes, "That very Spirit intercedes with sighs too deep for words" (Rom. 8:26). Listen to the sighing of the Spirit in this person or moving in you for this person. The Spirit's prayer may only be a few words such as "Be with me," "Peace," "Take courage." Join the Spirit in praying this prayer.

   Place your hand on the part of your body that you associate (physically or symbolically) with this person's need for God's healing or strengthening or renewal. Breathe in the warm light of God's healing love. Breathe out any pain, despair, or burden.

6. Now return to being yourself. Release the other person into God's hands. Place the right shoe back in the middle; retrieve and put on your own shoe.

Solitary reflection (reflection sheet) (3 minutes)
Invite everyone to spend three minutes reflecting with the aid of the Reflection Sheet on their experience of listening in prayer to the groans of pain and hope within *(a)* themselves (left shoe), *(b)* the other person (right shoe), and *(c)* the Spirit of God.

Mutual Listening in Pairs (5 minutes)
Ask everyone to pair up and take turns listening to one another express what he or she heard and experienced. (2 to 3 minutes each)

Group Reflection (5 minutes)
Lead the group in brief reflection on:

(a) the gift and the challenge of this exercise

(b) where they were most/least aware of God's presence during the meeting

CLOSING (10 MINUTES)

Reread aloud Trevor Hudson's prayer at the conclusion of his article (page 49, Participant's Book) as a way of leading the group into an awareness of God's prayer for us and for all people.

Ask: **What is the Spirit praying for us, in us?**

Silent prayer

Voiced prayer—Invite the group to voice expressions (as the Spirit leads them) of what they sense is God's prayer for us, for others, for the world.

Sing a closing hymn.

> Traditional: "Come, Ye Sinners, Poor and Needy" (UMH #340)

> Contemporary: "Kum Ba Yah" (UMH #494)

Check plans for the Closing Pilgrimage and Retreat. At the group's announcement time, call for an update from each of the five planning areas for the Pilgrimage and Retreat. By this time the retreat and pilgrimage sites should be chosen, reserved, and/or confirmed with the appropriate contact persons. Ask for a report on plans for meals and pass sign-up sheets if necessary to confirm who will bring food and supplies. If any major aspects of planning remain uncertain, request an estimate of the completion date.

Handout

SHOE PRAYER REFLECTION SHEET

1. Solitary reflection on the Shoe Prayer experience

   • What were the groans of pain and hope within yourself (left shoe)?

   • What were the groans of pain and hope you heard from the other person (right shoe)? What would it be like to walk for a day in his or her shoes?

   • What were the groans of pain and hope you heard from the Spirit of God? What new insight or idea was conceived in you by the Spirit? What message in it sounded like good news?

2. Mutual listening in pairs

   • Find a conversation partner. Take turns listening to each other express what you heard and experienced. (2–3 minutes each)

3. Group reflection

   • As you return to the group, take a few images or words that capture your experience during this intercessory prayer exercise and reflection. Be prepared to answer the following:

     – What was the gift and the challenge of this exercise?

     – Where were you most or least aware of God's presence during the meeting?

Week 4
Experiencing the God Who Heals

PREPARATION

Prepare yourself spiritually. This week identify the places in your own life that need healing, and ask for Christ's mercy. Read the article for Week 4 and complete the daily exercises, noting your insights in your journal. Pray for healing among the members of your *Companions* group, and for healing in your faith community and the world. Seek courage and wisdom from God as you prepare to lead the weekly meeting.

Prepare materials and the meeting space.

- Set up the meeting space with chairs in a circle, preferably around a small table at the center covered with a simple cloth. At the start of the meeting the table will be empty except for the cloth cover.

- The group will set the altar with five items during the opening litany. You will need a stone (or a container of soil), a plant (a potted plant or freshly cut flowers), a container of water, a single candle, and a container of oil, which will also be used for anointing during the Deeper Explorations time. Use small pieces of pottery or other natural containers for the water and oil.

- Make copies of "Christian Practices of Healing" (page 62), "Quotations about Christian Healing" (page 63) and "A Celebration of the Healing Powers of God" (pages 64–65) for each participant.

- Consider three persons whom you will ask to serve as readers. Read over the directions for the litany in the Opening section below, and be prepared to explain the instructions to those you enlist to help.

- Choose hymns or songs for opening and closing worship, including songbooks or tape/CD as needed.

- Familiarize yourself with the Deeper Explorations in which participants will engage in laying on hands and anointing with oil.

- Write the following words on a board or poster paper: *(Name), I anoint you and pray for healing in the name of Jesus Christ. Let this oil soak into your skin and remind you of the healing love of God.* Plan to display the words where everyone can see and use them during the Deeper Explorations.

DIRECTIONS FOR OPENING LITANY

1. Enlist three readers to help with the litany.

2. Enlist five people to carry the elements to the altar at the appropriate time. The following phrases signal the time to take each element to the altar:
   - "We celebrate the earth . . ." (carry the rock or stone to the altar)
   - "O God, your earth . . ." (carry the plant or flowers to the altar)
   - "O God, the waters . . ." (the container of water)
   - "O God, the fires . . ." (the lighted candle)
   - "the balm of healing oil . . ." (the container of oil)

   If your group is small, some people may need to do more than one task.

3. Ask everyone to read together the parts marked "All Voices."

Review the intent of this meeting: To notice the wounded places in one's self and to experience the healing power of God's presence and compassion through a caring community.

OPENING (10 MINUTES)

Greet each person and extend a welcome to the circle as everyone gathers.

Set a context.

In today's meeting we are invited to experience the healing presence of God through worship, sharing our insights and offering sacramental compassionate touch to one

another. We will open our time together with a litany that celebrates God's many healing powers.

Join together in worship.

* Read the following quotation from Joan Sauro about how God is present in all the layers of our lives. She says:

> God is in the fierce wind, the season of struggle, and in bountiful times, when life and goodness overflow within you. In every season of your life, God is with you in every layer.

> Most of all, though, God is in the worn, embattled, broken-down layers, because God always loved the poor and the weak. This is where to look for God most in yourself—where you are broken and vulnerable. Where you are scarred and need divine healing.[1]

* Ask:

> Where are you broken, vulnerable, scarred, and in need of divine healing? Allow a time of silent reflection.

* Say:

> The power and mystery of God's healing are all around us. Let us worship together and celebrate God's fearfully and wonderfully made creation.

* Distribute "A Celebration of the Healing Powers of God" (pages 64–65), and read the litany together, setting the altar as directed.

* Sing one of the following hymns or a song of your own choosing:
  Traditional: "God of Grace and God of Glory" (UMH #577)
  Contemporary: "Christ Beside Me" (TFWS # 2166)
  Taizé: "Come and Fill Our Hearts" (TFWS #2157)

SHARING INSIGHTS (45 MINUTES)

In Sharing Insights group members identify and share the ways they have experienced God's presence this week. The focus is on the insights they discovered while reading this week's article and doing the daily exercises. Remind the group again of this week's theme: receiving and offering God's healing grace through a caring community.

1. Ask participants to review the article and the notes they made in their journals. *(5 minutes)*

2. Invite group members to share insights from the reading. Invite deep listening to each person who shares and attention to the wisdom of God in the sharing process. Begin the sharing time from your own insights and experience of the presence of God this week. *(35 minutes)*

3. Conclude by asking the group to identify together what they sensed during the sharing time that seemed to them the wisdom of God's Spirit. *(5 minutes)*

Break (10 minutes)

Deeper Explorations (45 minutes)

Introduce the theme of Christian healing. (20 minutes total)

This Deeper Exploration is focused on healing grace and the means by which we become for one another a healing community in the church. We are going to practice expressions or means of grace (those means through which God gives grace), which the church has handed down and used for centuries to convey Christ's healing and renewing presence to those who are open to receive it.

Engage in a brief discussion of the nature of Christian healing. (10 minutes)

Invite participants to read the quotes on the handout titled "Quotations about Christian Healing."

• Invite people to identify images or phrases from these quotations they find particularly meaningful and explain why.

• Name some questions that these quotations raise:

What is keeping you from being fully alive? What is preventing you from letting your light shine or keeping you from allowing the glory of God to shine through you more fully? Where is your point of deepest need? At what place are your defenses the weakest? Where is the brokenness and pain in your soul?

• Allow time for reflection. Then say:

Whatever our responses to these questions, they point us to where we need God's healing grace and where Christ is prepared to meet us.

Introduce Christian practices of healing grace. (10 minutes)

In the James 5:13-20 passage that we worked with this week, we find several early church traditions or practices that express Christ's healing presence with and for one another:

– prayer (verse 13)
– singing (verse 13)
– calling on elders for assistance (verse 14)
– anointing with oil (verse 14)
– confessing sins to one another (verses 15 and 16).

Another healing practice of the early church is:

– laying on of hands (Mark 5:23)

There are other means of grace as well, including sacraments, and since modern times all of these are observed in cooperation with medical science. Today we are going to have an opportunity to share the experience of healing touch through the laying on of hands and anointing with oil.

Describe briefly to the group what these practices involve and represent. See the handout "Christian Practices of Healing" for more information about the laying on of hands and anointing with oil.

Experience Christ's healing touch. (25 minutes total)

Mark 3:1-6 is the story of Jesus healing a man with a withered hand. We are going to explore this story and let it lead us to name our woundedness and to ask for the healing we need.

Read Mark 3:1-6. (2 minutes)

In this reading, go through the story slowly, letting the images sink in.

Reflect together on the story. (8 minutes)

Invite the group to discuss briefly what this story reveals about Christian healing and about the church as a healing community. Focus on what can be seen in the text directly or metaphorically. Draw insights from the story such as these:

• When Jesus walks into our churches, he sees people in need of healing and transformation.

- The man had to make several choices: to show up in synagogue despite being impaired, to come forward, to be vulnerable, and to do as Jesus said.

- Healing involves admitting your need in the company of others and stretching it out before God.

- Obstacles to grace grieve God, and Jesus wants us to clear them away.

- Sometimes, as with other institutions, the church itself gets in the way of God and needs healing. Jesus wants the church to be a healing place.

- A measure of all church traditions and functions is whether they really contribute to people's healing and wholeness as images of God.

Reflect individually on the story. (5 minutes)

As I read the story again, put yourself in the place of the man with the withered hand. Prayerfully listen with your eyes closed this time as Jesus commands the man, "Come forward. . . . Stretch out your hand." Imagine Jesus is addressing you.

Invite everyone to take a few moments to consider what their "withered hand" might be. The withered hand may represent some hurt in need of healing, a relationship that has been severed, a loss of vitality; or it may represent some dormant gift that God would like to revitalize and use for good in the world. A "withered hand" may be any aspect of their lives that need the healing and restoration Jesus offers.

Practice being a healing community for one another. (10 minutes)

- Stand in a circle around the table. Invite those in need of any kind of healing to stretch out their hand before the group as a symbolic acknowledgement of need and openness to God. Let them know they may remain silent or say a word or phrase that represents their need.

- *Laying on of hands*—Lead the group in reaching out and touching the person's outstretched "withered hand" as Christ would. Pray silently as a group for the person.

- *Anointing with oil*—Assist group members, taking turns one at a time, in anointing the person's hand with oil, saying these words (displayed where everyone can read them): "_(Name)_, I anoint you and pray for healing in the name of Jesus Christ. Let this oil soak into your skin and remind you of the healing love of God."

- Give everyone a chance, one by one, to stretch out his or her "withered hand" for healing. Also give as many as possible a chance to practice anointing with oil. Simply hand different persons the oil in silence. Assist them as needed. Any who choose to pass may do so.

Closing (10 minutes)

The story concludes, "He stretched it out, and his hand was restored."

Ask:

What do you imagine your "withered hand" looks like restored?

Lead the group in a time of guided prayer. Say the following, pausing where the ellipses appear for participants to pray silently.

As we first turn our hearts toward God in prayer, see with eyes of faith the wounded part of your life being restored. . . . Express your hope and joy to God and give thanks. . . . Now, lift to God the person on your right. Celebrate who they are becoming by the mysterious grace of God at work within that person. . . . Finally, lift to God in the same way the person on your left. . . . God, we offer deep thanks for your divine mercy, compassion, and healing, and we offer these prayers in the name of Christ. Amen.

Sing a closing song:

Traditional: "Just as I Am, Without One Plea" (UMH #357) or "It Is Well with

My Soul" (UMH #377)

Spiritual: "There Is a Balm in Gilead" (UMH #375)

Check plans for the Closing Pilgrimage and Retreat. Ask the group during announcement time about any loose ends related to the Closing Pilgrimage and Retreat. Ask those responsible for the site confirmation to call or e-mail the contact person at the pilgrimage site this coming week. Be sure all the plans still are a go and find out how many persons will be sharing in the meal. This number should be communicated to those making food arrangements.

Handout

CHRISTIAN PRACTICES OF HEALING

(a) *Laying on of hands*—Touching can say, *I care for you. I love you. I am in touch with you. You are not alone.* God is in touch with us through the body of Christ. We ask, "What would you say to Jesus that you need right now? May we place our hands on you and pray for you?" We place our hands upon another person's head, shoulders, or hurt spot as we pray, offering our hands to Christ. We remain silent for a moment, then say a brief word of prayer expressing the person's request. We must make certain that when we practice laying on of hands, our attitude and actions are respectful and loving, not coercive or forced.

(b) *Anointing with oil*—Oil was a symbol of divine blessing and was a common medicinal remedy in ancient times. Anointing with oil has long served as a sign of God's healing and empowerment for a holy service. We ask, "May we anoint you with oil, as an outward sign of God's healing grace at work in you?" With a finger that has touched the oil, we make a sign of the cross on the person's forehead or hand. As we do so, we say words such as these: "(Name), I anoint you and pray for healing in the name of Jesus Christ. Let this oil soak into your skin and remind you of the healing love of God."

Anointing often accompanies laying on of hands. Anointing can also represent the gift of the Holy Spirit resting upon persons sent in the service of the Lord in some way.

Handout

QUOTATIONS ABOUT CHRISTIAN HEALING

- Trevor Hudson says, *"The simplest definition of the healing ministry of the Christian gospel is this: Jesus Christ meets us at the point of our deepest need"* (page 58, Participant's Book).

- Tilda Norberg in *Stretch Out Your Hand* says: *"Christian healing is a process that involves the totality of our being—body, mind, emotion, spirit, and our social context—and that directs us toward becoming the person God is calling us to be at every stage of our living and our dying. Whenever we are truly open to God, some kind of healing takes place, because God yearns to bring us to wholeness. Through prayer and the laying on of hands, through confession, anointing, the sacraments, and other means of grace, Jesus meets us in our brokenness and pain and there loves, transforms, forgives, redeems, resurrects, and heals. Jesus does this in God's way, in God's time, and according to God's loving purpose for each person."*[a]

- Bishop Irenaeus of Lyons in the second century said: *"[Human beings] fully alive is the glory of God."*[b]

- In writing about the places where divine healing is needed, Sister Joan Sauro says, *"Look for God where your defense is weakest. At the breach in the wall. The crack in the earth. The ground shifting out of control. Go to the place called barren. Stand in the place called empty. And you will find God there. . . . God always breaks through at your weakest point, where you least resist."*[c]

---

a. Tilda Norberg and Robert D. Webber, *Stretch Out Your Hand: Exploring Healing Prayer* (Nashville, Tenn.: Upper Room Books, 1998), 26.

b. Irenaeus, *Against Heresies* (Lib. 4, 20, 5–7; SC 100, 640–42, 644–48).

c. Joan Sauro, C.S.J., "The Whole Earth Meditation" in *The Weavings Reader: Living with God in the World*, ed. John Mogabgab (Nashville, Tenn.: Upper Room Books, 1993), p. 182.

Handout

A CELEBRATION OF THE HEALING POWERS OF GOD

by Eileen Campbell-Reed

All voices: **O Great Creator, you fill the earth with the richness of your bounty!**

Reader 1: You give us gifts of fire and water, earth and wind, every growing thing and the very breath of life.

Reader 2: We celebrate the earth that supports us, grounds us in the goodness of your creation, and daily gives us a place to stand. Yet we fear the earth when it shakes and trembles, slides and crashes into devastation and ruin.

Reader 3: The earth holds the mysteries of the ages and yields all that is needed to live and eat and heal our bodies.

All voices: **O God, your earth is fearfully and wonderfully made!**

Reader 1: We celebrate the gift of water that delights our senses, washes us clean, and quenches our thirst.

Reader 2: We are awed by the vastness of oceans, the power of hurricanes, the sweeping destruction of floods.

Reader 3: Water renews and heals in a single tear of grief, in the sweat and toil of hard work, and in the breaking waters of new birth.

All Voices: **O God, the waters flowing through creation are fearfully and wonderfully made!**

Reader 1: We celebrate the power of fire that purifies precious metal, warms us by night, and lights our way in the darkness.

Reader 2: Yet we stand in trepidation at a fire out of control, a volcano erupting, lightning that dances across the sky.

(Continued on next page)

(Continued from previous page)

Reader 3: A single spark gives us hope; a fire in the hearth invites us in, warms our hands and cooks the meal, while the burning sun sustains all growth and life.

All Voices: **O God, the fires that light creation are fearfully and wonderfully made!**

Reader 1: We celebrate the bounty of living things welling up in abundance upon the earth: every green and growing thing, land that flows with milk and honey, the balm of healing oil. We celebrate the richness of life that creeps and crawls, flies and swims, moves and has its breath in you.

Reader 2: Each good and perfect gift can be used for healing or harm, and we tremble in the face of good gifts turned to idols or squandered for evil.

Reader 3: Even we, your people, who are created and creative in your image, still find ourselves tragic and flawed, suffering and grieving, and in need of your healing powers.

All Voices: **O God, we celebrate all of creation, for it is fearfully and wonderfully made!**

"A Celebration of the Healing Powers of God" by Eileen Campbell-Reed. Copyright © 2005. Used by permission of the author.

Week 5

Discovering Community Together

PREPARATION

Prepare yourself spiritually. This week is the last session, with exception of the closing retreat. Think back over the weeks you have shared and give thanks for ways God has been present. Read the article for Week 5 and complete the daily exercises, recording insights, ideas, and promptings from the Spirit in your journal. Pray for members of your *Companions* group and the larger faith community. Ask for God's wisdom and guidance as you prepare to lead the weekly meeting.

Prepare materials and the meeting space.

- If possible, plan to hold this week's meeting in your church building (even if you typically meet in a home or other setting).

- Arrange for access into the various areas of your building for the prayer walk, which is the focus of the Deeper Exploration. For this activity you will need one additional portable candle or small lamp to take with you on the prayer walk.

- Plan the path you will take through your building, especially if other groups are meeting at the same time.

- Set up your meeting space with chairs in a circle, preferably around a small table at the center, covered with a simple cloth.

- Place on the table the Christ candle. Also place on the altar one smaller candle (a votive will work nicely) for each member of your group.

- If you plan to use the Candle Prayer (see page 19), display the poster.

- Choose hymns or songs for opening and closing worship, including songbooks or tape/CD as needed.

- Be sure to give participants information about the Closing Pilgrimage and Retreat (date, time, location, what to bring).

Review the intent of this meeting: To celebrate the gift of God's presence in the life and relationships of the faith community and to seek a deeper sense of shared life together by opening in prayer to the leading of the Spirit.

OPENING (10 MINUTES)

Welcome each person by name as people arrive.

Set a context.

> This is our last weekly meeting for *The Way of Transforming Discipleship.* Appropriately, we conclude with a focus on discovering community. The Christian life cannot be lived in isolation. Christ calls us into community with all its choices, messy conflicts, strangeness, and failures, as well as its moments of grace, forgiveness, hope, and glimpses of sacredness.

Join together in worship.

- Light the candle and say the Candle Prayer together or offer a prayer of thanksgiving for life together in Christian community.

- Read the following quotation from Robert Morris:

  > "The biblical mandate to welcome the stranger comes with the promise that we may be blessed by unexpected grace. . . . Hospitality to strangers may lead not only to 'entertaining angels without knowing it' (Heb. 13:2), but also to encountering the Divine itself in disguise (Matt. 25:35)."[1]

- Invite participants to reflect on the following questions:
  - Where in the last few weeks of our journey together have you experienced grace in a surprising or unexpected way?
  - Where have you encountered the divine in our companionship, spiritual practice, and fellowship?

- Allow time for brief responses.

- Invite sentence prayers of thanksgiving for the experiences you named together.

- Sing one of the following or a song of your own choosing.

Traditional: "One Bread, One Body" (UMH #620)

Contemporary: "The Servant Song" (TFWS #2222)

SHARING INSIGHTS (45 MINUTES)

In this portion of the meeting, group members identify and share ways they have experienced God's presence while reading this week's article and doing the daily exercises. Remind the group again of this week's theme: To discover community together means sharing genuine fellowship (*koinonia*), relating to God and each other by walking in the light, and opening up to the Spirit in order that we might receive the gift of a shared life together.

1. Ask participants to review the article and the notes they made in their journals. (*5 minutes*)

2. Invite group members to share insights from the reading. Encourage deep listening for the presence of Christ in the stories and experiences of their companions. Begin the sharing time from your own insights and experience of the presence of God this week. (*35 minutes*)

3. Conclude the time by asking the group to name together the moments of genuine community, or *koinonia*, which they experienced in the sharing time. (*5 minutes*)

BREAK (10 MINUTES)

DEEPER EXPLORATIONS (45 MINUTES)

Set a context. (10 minutes)

The focus of this Deeper Exploration is Trevor Hudson's question, "Jesus, where do you hang out in this church?"

• Ask someone to read 1 John 1:5-7.

• Ask the group rhetorically,

Where does Jesus hang out in this church? And what is Jesus happiest about in the quality of fellowship going on here?

• *Explain the prayer walk through the church.*

The group will be taking a prayer walk through the church building. (If all of the spaces are being used by other groups, it is possible to do this prayer practice as an act of imagination, picturing each space as you pray.)

As we are walking along through this brief journey, you are invited to pray silently for all the life, love, need, change, disagreement, decision, hope, and communion that takes place when we are gathered here.

- Tell them that upon entering each space the group will respond to three questions, then you will call for a volunteer to offer a prayer. The questions:

  - **What happens in this space?**

  - **Who are the people who gather, worship, work, visit, clean, sing, play, study, or teach in this space?**

  - **In what ways is Christ present in this space?**

We will carry this candle (or lamp) with us throughout our prayer walk as a symbol of our desire to walk in the light and to be in true fellowship with one another and the Spirit of Christ.

Take a prayer walk through your church building. (30 minutes)

Follow the route you have planned in advance through the church. For time's sake, if your church building is large, you can choose representative spaces rather than going to every room (for example, stop in one classroom to represent all teaching spaces). In smaller churches some spaces may have multiple functions. You can address this by focusing the three questions on specific functions. If other groups are meeting or gathering in some rooms, you may be able to gather outside the space and offer your reflection and prayers without any interruption.

Spaces to visit:

- sanctuary or worship spaces
- kitchen
- fellowship spaces
- classrooms
- children's or play areas
- youth areas

- offices
- outdoor spaces
- music and art spaces
- storage, supply, and work areas
- library or study spaces

Pray for the church. (5 minutes)

- End your prayer walk back in your *Companions* room, giving thanks for your small group and the presence of Christ that has been with you throughout these recent weeks.

- Lead a time of additional reflection with these questions:
  - **Where did you sense Christ's presence as we walked?**
  - **As we went from space to space, remembering what happens in each space (including our own here), what were the qualities of fellowship that Jesus was most at home with, happiest about being part of or present for?**
  - **Imagine Jesus had actually taken the walk with us. What would he say to us (and our church) now by way of encouragement or challenge?**

- Invite participants to offer prayers for unity and shared life by coming to the altar table one by one and lighting a candle. They may voice their prayers or offer them silently.

CLOSING (10 MINUTES)

Pass the peace of Christ.

Set a context.

> Over the past five weeks together we have learned about and attempted various practices of faith. As we bring our meeting and our series of weekly meetings to a close, we are going to experience yet one more common practice of Christian fellowship and worship. We are going to pass the peace of Christ among ourselves. Often the openings and closings of New Testament letters offer the peace of Christ as a blessing from the writer to the readers. (See, for example, Rom. 1:7; Gal. 1:3; Eph. 6:23; 2 John 1:3.)

Remind group members of the common refrain for passing the peace: One person says, "The peace of Christ be with you"; and the other responds, "And also with you." Invite everyone to take time to greet each person with the peace of Christ and to offer a few other words of thanks and encouragement for time spent together in the past five weeks. The time of passing the peace is most often accompanied by handshakes, warm hugs, and on occasion the exchange of a holy kiss of peace.

When the group has offered the peace of Christ to each other, gather the group into a circle and join hands. Close the time by singing a benediction.

Traditional: "I Want to Walk as a Child of the Light" (UMH #206)

Contemporary: "They'll Know We Are Christians by Our Love" (TFWS #2223)

Check plans for the Closing Pilgrimage and Retreat.

Before leaving today, distribute a revised schedule for the weekend's Closing Pilgrimage and Retreat. Ask for any final needs or instructions from each area: Food, Site Selection, Transportation, Meeting Facilitation, and Worship. Remind everyone that although they have no article to read for the coming week, they do have daily exercises in the Participant's Book to help them prepare for the event. Also remind them to bring their journals to the Closing Pilgrimage and Retreat.

Closing Pilgrimage and Retreat

PURPOSE

The closing event for *The Way of Transforming Discipleship* gives participants an experience of pilgrimage into the suffering, need, and hope in their own communities. It will also provide retreat time to reflect on the shared experiences of the previous six weeks, as well as time to process and debrief the pilgrimage itself.

Specific purpose and requests:
- to visit as pilgrims (not missionaries or tourists)
- to be with the people for part of a day (3–4 hours) and hear their stories
- to talk with leaders and caregivers who attend to the suffering
- to share a simple meal
- to do no harm

Possible pilgrimage sites:
- homeless shelter or day shelter for homeless persons
- community center in an impoverished section of town
- church-based programs that care for the poor, homeless, or other groups in need
- domestic violence or teenage runaway shelters
- rehabilitation center for those in recovery from addictions

ADVANCE PREPARATION

Preparing spiritually. The daily exercises and weekly meetings serve to prepare participants for the Closing Pilgrimage and Retreat by introducing important concepts, inviting prayer and deep listening, and practicing the disciplines that open persons to new experiences. Additionally, it will be important for everyone in the group to pray specifically for the pilgrimage and for those who will be encountered in this brief journey. It will also be helpful to remind participants that while we can plan for many things, we cannot control all factors or ensure particular outcomes of a pilgrimage. A certain spiritual detachment, or freedom from worry about how we will be received, facilitates opening to the movement of the Spirit. To help with this posture and spirit of pilgrimage, a set of daily exercises has been developed for the week leading up to the Closing Pilgrimage and Retreat. They are found on pages 77–81 of the Participant's Book. Participants should continue the daily practice of prayer and journal keeping up to the time of the event. If possible, schedule the Closing Pilgrimage and Retreat on the next weekend following the last weekly meeting.

Prepare materials and the meeting space(s). A variety of tasks will need to be accomplished to make the Closing Pilgrimage and Retreat a meaningful experience. In order to get these things done, the following divisions of labor are recommended. Everyone in your small group should be assigned to work on one of the tasks. Enlist volunteers during the Preparatory Meeting when the group gathers for the first time. The task descriptions can be photocopied and shared with group members. During each weekly meeting, check in to see how tasks are progressing.

THE WAY OF TRANSFORMING DISCIPLESHIP
CLOSING PILGRIMAGE AND RETREAT SCHEDULE OUTLINE

FRIDAY EVENING

6:00	Gather for dinner (potluck or other simple fare)
7:00	Opening worship
7:15	Sharing insights from the week
8:00	Overview of the pilgrimage site and plans for Saturday
8:15	Deeper Explorations
9:00	Evening prayers
9:15	Sending forth

SATURDAY MORNING

8:00	Morning prayers (coffee, tea, or juice may be made available)
8:30	Travel to the pilgrimage site
9:00	Meet with residents and caregivers at the site
12:00	Shared lunch at the pilgrimage site
1:00	Return travel to the retreat site
1:30	Individual reflection and journaling time
2:15	Group reflection
3:10	Letter writing
3:45	Closing worship and communion or Love Feast
4:15	Sending forth

SITE SELECTION AND PERMISSION

This task has two parts: securing a site for the preparation and retreat portions of the gathering and securing a site for the pilgrimage portion of the gathering.

Retreat Site — This site could be your church facility or a member's home. Depending on where you decide the pilgrimage will take place, the retreat portions of the meeting could also be held at the pilgrimage site if adequate space is available and secured. The times for the preparation and retreat include several hours on Friday evening, Saturday morning, and several hours on Saturday afternoon. (See the retreat schedule outline for more detailed information.) Whatever location you choose, reserve it on appropriate calendars, arrange to get in, set up the space, and leave it as clean as you found it.

Pilgrimage Site — This site will be the more challenging one to secure. Start by getting input from your *Companions* group about sites members think would be good for the pilgrimage (see possible suggestions below). When you have selected a potential site, identify a contact person and call or visit to explain your purpose and requests (see below). Describe the size of your group and suggest the date you would like to come. Offer to share a simple meal that your *Companions* group might either provide or work with people there to make and share. Ask who might be available to meet with you—recipients of services, neighborhood residents, and caregivers. When the date and time have been agreed upon, work with the contact person at the pilgrimage site to sketch out a schedule for your visit. Determine how you will spend the three to four hours (seeing specific program components, speaking one-on-one or in group conversations, eating, or other activities appropriate to the site).

Specific purpose and requests:
- to visit as pilgrims (not missionaries or tourists)
- to be with the people for part of a day (3–4 hours) and hear their stories
- to talk with leaders and caregivers who attend to the suffering
- to share a simple meal
- to do no harm

*Specific things **not** to do:*
- to understand this visit as a charity or mission project
- to act as tourists or voyeurs at the expense of others
- to assume that we already know what we might see or learn

Possible pilgrimage sites:
- homeless shelter or day shelter for homeless persons
- community center in an impoverished section of town
- church-based programs that care for the poor, homeless, or other groups in need
- domestic violence or teenage runaway shelters
- rehabilitation center for those in recovery from addictions

TRANSPORTATION ARRANGEMENTS

Once the sites have been selected, your task is to arrange transportation (if needed) between the retreat and pilgrimage sites. You might reserve your church bus or van, arrange for carpooling, or plan to take public transportation. Estimate the travel times, make sure everyone has directions, and see that vehicles are reserved (if necessary). Communicate with the group, and specifically with the worship leader(s) and meeting facilitator(s), if the schedule needs adjusting based on the transportation times. And keep in mind that you may also need to transport food.

FOOD ARRANGEMENTS

Keep all arrangements for food simple so that they are neither a distraction from the overall purpose of the Closing Pilgrimage and Retreat nor a burden for the participants. Adapt the following suggestions to the needs of your group and the pilgrimage site.

Friday dinner — potluck brought by all members or other simple fare

Saturday morning — coffee, tea, and juice for the gathering time, and if the group chooses, muffins, pastries, or fruit

Saturday lunch — Coordinate with the contact person at the pilgrimage site because your *Companions* group and those at the site will share this meal. You might offer to bring ingredients for sandwiches that the groups could assemble together; or you may prefer to collect money from the *Companions* group and order food such as pizza; or you might decide to bring a potluck meal. Make sure the decision is agreeable to the contact person at the pilgrimage site, and get a count of how many people will be eating, so you can provide plenty of food. Also be sure that the necessary plates, cups, drinks, and utensils are available, or plan to bring them.

WORSHIP AND MUSIC

Worship takes place four times during the Closing Pilgrimage and Retreat: Opening Worship, Evening Prayers, Morning Prayers, and Closing Communion. For the morning and evening prayers you may prefer to use a worship book from your own tradition. Some suggestions for these times are included in the detailed outline for the retreat. Other specific details should be planned and led or delegated by you. A basic list of items needed follows here.

Items needed

- Small table and simple cloth to serve as the altar for the worship times
- Christ candle
- Recorded music and tape or CD player and printed words or other means for leading or accompanying music
- Extra Bibles
- Elements for communion or Love Feast, including a chalice or cup, juice or wine, a plate, and a loaf of bread
- *Optional:* Prayer/Worship books; Communion or Love Feast liturgies

MEETING FACILITATION

As the facilitator of the meeting, look in advance at the detailed outline for the Closing Pilgrimage and Retreat, coordinating with those who will lead worship times. You will be responsible for guiding participants through the various aspects of the experience, much like the leader of weekly meetings.

Items needed

For Friday:

- Newsprint and markers or chalkboard/whiteboard
- On four pieces of newsprint or across the whiteboard write these four headings—"preparation," "encounter," "reflection," "transformation"—leaving room to write below each heading.

For Saturday:

- Newsprint and markers or chalkboard/whiteboard
- Write the following questions on newsprint or whiteboard and display in the retreat area:

    - "What did you learn, experience, or discover that could make a difference for you, the church, or the world?"

    - "With whom would you find joy by sharing some of your experience?"

    - "Who would find joy in hearing it?"

- Blank paper for the letter-writing exercise

THE WAY OF TRANSFORMING DISCIPLESHIP
CLOSING PILGRIMAGE AND RETREAT

FRIDAY EVENING

6:00   Gather for dinner (potluck or other simple fare)

7:00   Opening worship

- Invite silence for centering/adoration; meditative music optional

- Light the Christ candle and say words to the following effect:

    We are gathered in the living presence of Christ once again. Our retreat and tomorrow's pilgrimage mark the end of this *Companions* **experience but not the end of our being companions in Jesus Christ. We are not pilgrims alone but have been learning the profound value of companionship for the journey. Through the experiences of this weekend we will have a chance to reflect on where we have come by God's grace and ways we may be changing in response to our time together. Through this evening's retreat time we will prepare ourselves for tomorrow's pilgrimage of pain and hope. Tomorrow we will reflect on our experiences and contemplate ways we might continue our spiritual journeys and share them with our larger faith community.**

- Sing or play a hymn or song. Suggestion: "Be Thou My Vision" (UMH #451)

- Read a Psalm of praise, followed by silence

- Offer a prayer of gratitude for what the time in *The Way of Transforming Discipleship* has meant, and ask that God's purpose be fulfilled in each person present and the congregation(s) represented

- Say a brief benediction

7:15   Sharing insights from the week

- *Set a context.*

    Over the last several weeks together we have spent considerable time in the work of sharing insights with one another about the ways we have experienced God's presence. This evening we will also share the insights we've had while completing the daily exercises this past week.

- Ask participants to review the notes they made in their journals this week. To stimulate thinking you might ask the following questions:

    – **What, if any, transformations do you sense at work in you in these past few weeks?**

    – **What have you identified as anticipation or anxiety related to tomorrow's pilgrimage?**

    – **What have you discovered about yourself as you practiced the skills of attentiveness to your surroundings?**

    – **When during these recent weeks did you find yourself experiencing a deeper awareness of God's presence?**

- Invite group members to share insights. Remind them that the task of those listening is to attend fully to each speaker without fixing, judging, or proselytizing. As the leader, begin the sharing time with your own experiences this week.

- Conclude by asking the group to identify common themes they heard in the sharing time.

8:00   Overview of the pilgrimage site and plans for Saturday

- Ask for a report from each of the groups assigned to care for details of Site Selection, Food, Transportation, Worship, and Meeting Facilitation.

- Make sure everyone knows where to be, what to bring, and what time to gather in the morning.

8:15   Deeper Explorations

- *Set a context.*

> Together we have been planning a pilgrimage that will take place tomorrow. It will be a brief encounter with people suffering in our city (county, or region). Following the direction of Trevor Hudson who has been guiding us in these weeks, we might think of the process we are now sharing in four parts: preparation, encounter, reflection, and transformation. As we have noted before, we can plan, pray, encounter, and even reflect, but none of these things guarantee transformation. Instead, transformation is a gift that we hope for and sometimes see only in hindsight.

> As part of our preparation for tomorrow's pilgrimage, let's explore the wisdom of a New Testament story to see what it tells us about preparation, encounter, reflection, and transformation.

- *Read Luke 24:13-35 slowly for the group.* Ask people to listen for instances of *preparation, encounter, reflection,* and *transformation* as the story is read. Then work together as a group to list on the board or newsprint what you heard related to each phase of this process of pilgrimage. The following ideas may stimulate discussion if needed.

    - *Preparation* — These disciples had been with Jesus for some time; they knew from firsthand experience about his teaching, his healing, and all the events of recent days including his trial and crucifixion; they had been preparing for this encounter for a long time, although they may not have realized it fully until looking back.

    - *Encounter* — The two disciples had a profound encounter with pain and hope over just the past week; make a list of the personal pains they must have felt and the suffering of others they witnessed; describe the hope they held; describe their encounter with the stranger on the road in the midst of their deep suffering and grief.

    - *Reflection* — They recounted to the stranger what they had seen and heard; they reflected with the stranger as he told them biblical stories and shed new light on them; the disciples reflected with each other; they broke bread together and in that act their eyes were opened; they noticed their feelings (burning hearts) when they looked back at the walk with the stranger on the Emmaus road.

- *Transformation*—Note what seemed to be the key to the disciples' transformation: encountering and recognizing the living Christ; also note what happened when they experienced a change of feeling, attitude, and understanding: they got up and ran back to the city—the place of pain and suffering—with renewed hope, and there they encountered the risen Christ again.

- Ask the following:

   What can we learn from this New Testament story for our pilgrimage tomorrow?

   Spend a few moments drawing connections to the anticipated pilgrimage. Use the following questions to guide discussion:

   - How have our lives and the last six weeks been preparing us for tomorrow?

   - How might our encounters with strangers turn out to be encounters with Christ?

   - How can we attend deeply to the situation and the people we will meet?

- Invite a time of intercessory prayer for the group, individuals in the group, the people you will meet tomorrow, and the complex systems of pain and suffering that make this pilgrimage important.

9:00   Evening prayers
- Select song, scripture, prayer, and blessing; or use an evening prayer service from your tradition

9:15   Sending forth

SATURDAY MORNING

8:00   Morning prayers (coffee, tea, or juice may be offered)

- Silence, scripture, prayer, song, blessing; or use a morning prayer service from your tradition

8:30   Travel to the pilgrimage site

9:00   Meet with clients or residents and caregivers at the site

(Fill in this part of the schedule with the details of your particular pilgrimage.)

12:00   Shared lunch at the pilgrimage site

1:00   Return travel to the retreat site

1:30   Individual reflection and journaling time

- When the group returns to the retreat site, invite members to spend time in personal reflection and writing in their journals. Ask them to record what they noticed as they attended to the place, the people, and the circumstances of the pilgrimage. Ask them also to record what they noticed about their own reactions, feelings, and inner experiences while they were at the pilgrimage site. And finally, ask them to write down what they noticed about God's presence, promptings, or nudges while they were there. In other words, ask them to listen deeply to the situation and the people, to themselves, and to God's Spirit.

2:15   Group reflection

- Call participants back to the whole group and debrief your experiences together.
- Light the Christ candle and offer a prayer for open hearts and minds.

- Set a context for reflection.

  Having been on many pilgrimages, Trevor Hudson observes that when we open our eyes and our lives to suffering persons, three things emerge: "The Spirit of God opens blind eyes, uncovers inner poverty, [and] reveals hidden riches."[1]

  As you reflect together, use the following two categories written on newsprint or markerboard:

  "Outer pain, poverty, suffering"   "Inner pain, poverty, suffering"

- Begin by naming what participants observed as the outer pain, poverty, and suffering in the situation. List them on the board. How were their eyes opened? How are they seeing the world differently? Then move to what these observations stirred in their own souls. What inner pain, poverty of spirit, or personal suffering did this experience reveal?

- Say:

  We have focused on the part of this pilgrimage that evoked pain and suffering, and we have attended to the ways we also share in that pain and suffering as part of God's creation. Now we want to spend time noticing what hidden riches were uncovered in this experience.

  Write the following two categories on newsprint or the board:

  "Hidden riches, joy, hope of others" "Hidden riches, joy, hope in us"

- Ask participants to name the riches of hope and joy that they witnessed at the pilgrimage site. Ask them what inner joy or hope it stirred in their own being. What new resources in their lives may have been called forth by this experience? What encouragement, healing, or transformation does this hope suggest?

- Say in your own words:

  Pilgrimage does not have to be a one-time, special event. The way of the pilgrim can be the daily way of life for a Christ-follower. Consider for a few moments what such a commitment to pilgrimage might mean for your life.

  Allow a time of silent reflection.

- Close the group reflection time with a period of prayer in which participants can pray aloud as the Spirit leads.

BREAK (10 MINUTES)

3:10   Letter writing

- *Set a context.*

    In 1 John 1:1-10, the author represents the voice of a faith community that seeks to include others in the joy of its fellowship through an act of faith sharing. Notice that the plural pronoun "we" is used four times in the opening verse. In this case, these Christians share their faith by writing a letter to a Christian community with which they seek a true fellowship by walking together the way of Christ.

- *Lead a brief discussion about faith sharing* (10 minutes)— as illustrated in the first chapter of 1 John and from their experience. Read the opening verses of John's letter (1 John 1:1-10), which illustrate faith sharing so well.

    – Ask the group:

        Based on this verse and your own experience, how would you describe what faith sharing is and is not? What do you see John doing here?

    – List responses on a whiteboard or newsprint. Here are some possible responses if you and the group need prompting:

        ▪ Faith sharing is concrete, not abstract; not someone else's ideas or story or statements of doctrine, but personal experience.

        ▪ It declares our actual experience of God: what we've seen and heard and touched.

        ▪ It invites people to receive our experience rather than telling them what they ought to believe.

        ▪ It shares our story of faith, our struggles and insights, and what difference Christ makes in our lives.

- ▪ Faith sharing is entirely honest and open about failures, the fact that we sin, and where we need God's grace for living.

- ▪ It deepens our conversation, connecting at the level of who we really are and what we are becoming in God.

- – Ask the group:

  Where have you experienced any of these things in the course of these recent weeks?

- • Invite the group to enter into a faith sharing exercise, first as individuals and then as a group.

  - – *Individual work* (15 minutes) — Provide blank paper for everyone. Say in your own words:

    You have been on a journey, on the way of transforming discipleship, with several other pilgrims for six weeks now. Imagine writing a letter to a group in the congregation or persons outside the faith community that begins, "I want to share with you what I've heard, seen with my own eyes, looked at, and discovered for myself concerning the real life of faith during a six-week journey on the way of transforming discipleship." What would the letter include? What would you say?

  - – Refer to the following questions that you printed earlier on newsprint: (see "Meeting Facilitation" page 79)

    - ▪ What did you learn, experience, or discover that could make a difference for you, the church, or the world?

    - ▪ With whom would you find joy by sharing some of your experience?

    - ▪ Who would find joy in hearing it?

  - – *Group work* (20 minutes) — As a group, go around the circle and invite everyone to share at least one response to the questions. Then challenge the group to write a faith-sharing letter to the church that communicates a gift and a challenge based on the group's experience.

- Silently meditate on these questions for one minute: **What has blessed us that would bless others as well? What would deepen or broaden the fellowship we have in Christ? What would I find joy in sharing, and with whom?**

- Lead the group in listing their responses and write a letter that expresses the voice of the group.

  - Ask someone to act as scribe and capture the key shared points of the group's insights.

  - Decide whom you are addressing.

  - Put the thoughts together in a letter format, beginning, for example, in the style of 1 John 1.

  - Read the letter aloud to the group, improve it, and celebrate it.

  - Decide where you want to read or publish it as an act of faith sharing. Be ready to offer leadership for a new *Way of Transforming Discipleship* group in your church.

3:45   Closing worship and communion or Love Feast

- Read scripture (Luke 24:28-35).

- Share in moment of silent reflection.

- Invite the group to a time of open-eyed prayers. Go around the circle so that each person can name what he or she is thankful for about the time of shared companionship and pilgrimage over the past six weeks.

- Use the communion liturgy from your tradition. A Love Feast service is found in *The United Methodist Book of Worship* (page 581–84) and online at http://www.gbod.org/worship.[2] Offer a blessing or the words of institution for the bread and cup.

- Share in Holy Communion by passing the elements around the circle. The first person should hold the plate and cup while the second person tears off bread, dips it in the cup, and eats. This way the group is sharing a common cup, symbolizing shared suffering and hope.

- Sing or say a benediction.

4:15   Sending forth

Notes

WEEK 2: CHANGING FROM THE INSIDE

1. Agnes Cunningham, "Alive to God in Christ Jesus," *Weavings* (July/August 2002): 35–36.

WEEK 3: LISTENING TO THE GROANS

1. Kristen Johnson Ingram, "Doing Prayer" *Weavings* (May/June 2002): 31.
2. "Open My Eyes, That I May See," lyrics by Clara H. Scott, *The United Methodist Hymnal* (Nashville, Tenn.: The United Methodist Publishing House, 1989), no. 454.
3. Madeleine L'Engle, *Walking on Water: Reflections on Faith & Art* (Wheaton, Ill.: Harold Shaw Publishers, 1972), 49, 22, 19.

WEEK 4: EXPERIENCING THE GOD WHO HEALS

1. Joan Sauro, CSJ, "The Whole Earth Meditation," *The Weavings Reader: Living with God in the World*, ed. John Mogabgab (Nashville, Tenn.: Upper Room Books, 1993), 182.

WEEK 5: DISCOVERING COMMUNITY TOGETHER

1. Robert Morris, "Fear or Fascination? God's Call in a Multicultural World," *Weavings* (September/October 2003): 21.

CLOSING PILGRIMAGE AND RETREAT

1. Trevor Hudson, *A Mile in My Shoes* (Nashville, Tenn.: Upper Room Books, 2005), 43.
2. "The Love Feast," *The United Methodist Book of Worship* (Nashville, Tenn.: The United Methodist Publishing House, 1992), 581–84.

Evaluation

When your group has completed *The Way of Transforming Discipleship* resource, share your insights and experiences. Copy this page if you prefer to keep it. Use additional paper if needed.

1. Describe your group's experience with *The Way of Transforming Discipleship*.

2. In what ways did the resource lead participants to a fuller understanding of spiritual formation and to a more experiential knowledge of spiritual practices? Please share your perceptions with us in this evaluation or through the discussion room at www.companionsinchrist.org.

3. What would improve *The Way of Transforming Discipleship*?

4. Do you have follow-up plans for your group? Do you plan to begin the twenty-eight-week *Companions in Christ* foundational course?

5. What other kinds of resources are you looking for? What other topics would you like to see in the *Companions in Christ* series?

Mail to: *Companions in Christ*
c/o Robin Pippin, Editorial Director
Upper Room Ministries
P.O. Box 340004
Nashville, TN 37203-0004
or FAX 615-340-1783

About the Author

Stephen D. Bryant is editor and publisher of Upper Room Ministries. His vision of small groups as important settings for spiritual formation and his experience in the contemplative life as well as local churches provided the inspiration for the Companions in Christ series. Stephen was instrumental in shaping the foundational twenty-eight-week *Companions* resource and continues to shape and co-write the subsequent resources in the series.

Before his election as editor and publisher, Stephen, an ordained minister and former pastor in The United Methodist Church, served as the Director of Spiritual Formation for The Upper Room and as the International Director of The Walk to Emmaus and Chrysalis movements. He holds a certificate in Theology of Christian Spirituality from Lehb Shomea House of Prayer in Sarita, Texas—a center for contemplative prayer and spiritual theology related to Oblate School of Theology in San Antonio, Texas. He studied with the Shalem Institute of Spiritual Formation.